Leadir kids club in your church

by
Vernon Cracknell

JBCE

The Joint Board of Christian Education
Melbourne

Published by
THE JOINT BOARD OF CHRISTIAN EDUCATION
Second Floor, 10 Queen Street, Melbourne 3000,
Australia

LEADING A KIDS CLUB IN YOUR CHURCH

National Library of Australia
    Cataloguing-in-Publication entry.

Cracknell, Vernon
    Leading a kids club in your church

    Bibliography.
    Includes index.
    ISBN 0 85819 795 2.

    1. Church work with children. 2. Christian leadership.
I. Joint Board of Christian Education. II. Title.

259.22

First printed 1990

Cover design by Kelvin Young
Design by Jennifer Wait
Typeset by Savage Type Pty Ltd
Printed by The Book Printer   JB90/1896

Contents

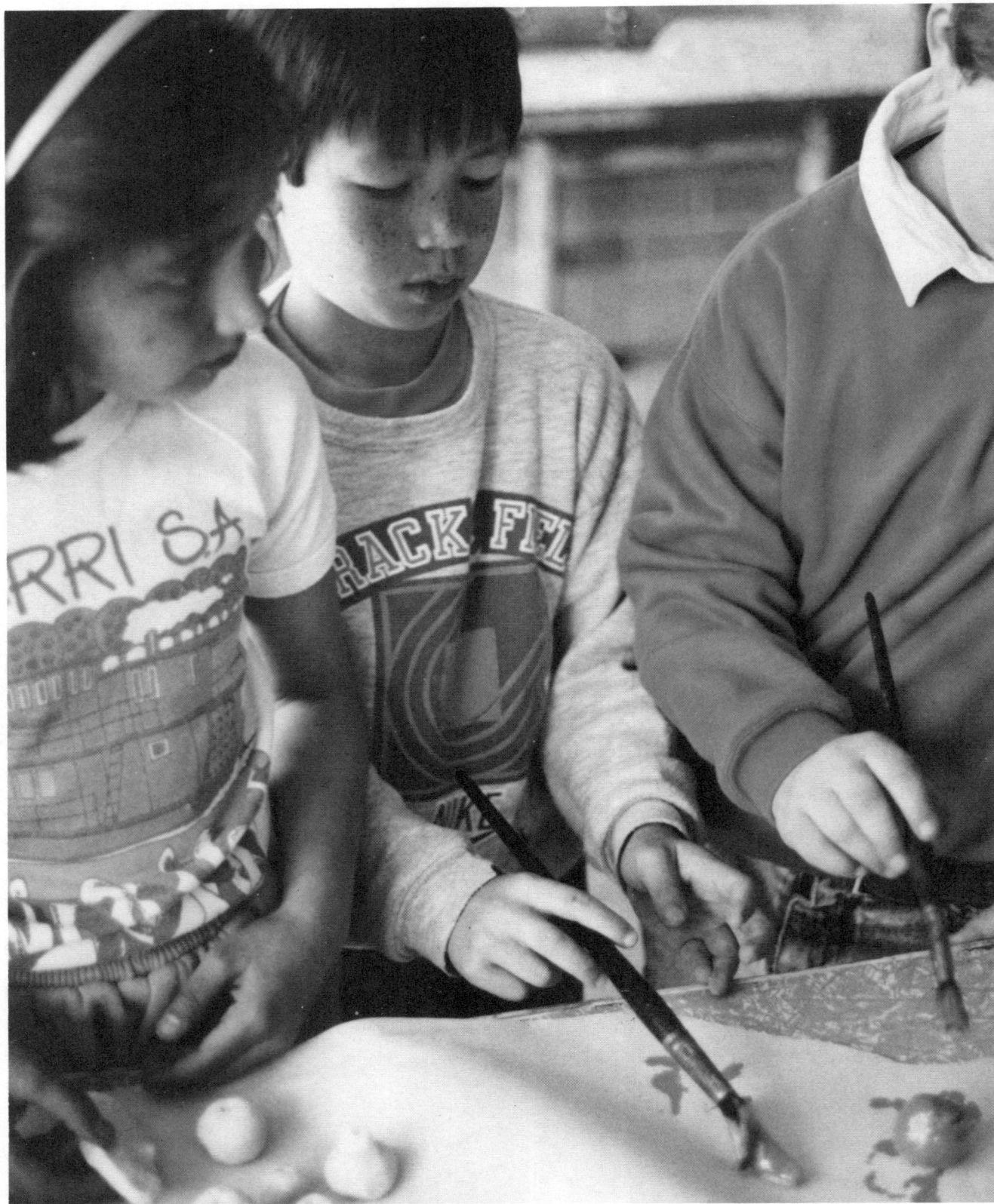

Acknowledgments

A project such as this can only be undertaken with goodwill in the church. I express my thanks to those who assisted in the research that provided the foundation information for this material.

Particularly I acknowledge the assistance of Gwen and Rex Coleman, Ros. Scott, Di Grimm, Margaret Baker, Margaret White, Judi Jones, Velma Beaglehole, Colleen Brooks, Nicki Cowan, Damien Trenorden, Bruce Stribley, Kay Gale, Sue Burt, Rev. Ian Lohmeyer, Ros. Byrne, Val Edwards, Bronte Wilson, Marg. Bartlett and Dean Trevan.

The particular help of a 'sounding board' group concerned with the questions of the theology of children's ministry is likewise acknowledged. To the Rev. Ken Anderson, Rev. Dr Laurie Mickan, Rev. David Houston, Heather Busch, and Russell Reynoldson I express gratitude for their interest, support and contributions.

The practical and moral support for the undertaking of this project by the Rev. Ken Anderson (when in the role as Consultant, Children's Youth and Young Adults Ministries, U.C.A.–S.A. Synod), Russell Reynoldson (Children's Worker, U.C.–S.A. Synod) and the Rev. Dr David Merritt (Executive Director, Joint Board of Christian Education) is enthusiastically recorded. I am grateful for the photographic support of Trevor Bartlett, and the co-operation of the leaders and children of the Westbourne Park Kids Club.

I gratefully acknowledge the support of Raeleen and our family through the various phases of the project.

Signposts

This book is not intended to be read through page by page like a novel. Rather you are invited to use the book in ways relevant to you as an individual. Here are some signposts that indicate useful approaches.

IF YOU ARE NEW TO CHILDREN'S CLUB WORK

You are beginning, perhaps, as a leader.

Step 1: Read the Introduction.

Step 2: Then choose as your first priority the learning program most relevant to you from Part 2.

Step 3: As you work with your mentor and use further materials from Part 2, begin to read in Part 1. Return to Part 1 regularly as your experience broadens.

IF YOU ARE EXPERIENCED IN CHILDREN'S CLUB WORK

Step 1: Read the Introduction.

Step 2: Then look at the learning program titles in Part 2. Choose one in which you want to build your experience. Ask your mentor to help.

Step 3: Read Part 1 along the way, and use its chapters to help you reflect on your experiences of club work.

IF YOU HAVE BEEN ASKED TO BE A MENTOR

Your learner-friend has asked you to be a mentor.

Step 1: Read the Introduction.

Step 2: Then read Part 3 with its two chapters.

Step 3: Then look through the learning program your friend wishes to work on first from Part 2.

Step 4: Then in between read Part 1 and the other programs in Part 2.

IF YOU ARE A TRAINER AND WILL BE ACTING AS A MENTOR FOR A TRAINING GROUP

Step 1: Read the Introduction.

Step 2: Read the material in Part 3 so that you are aware of the training method used in these training programs.

Step 3: Then establish the order in which the learning programs will be taken by the group.

Step 4: Then read Part 1 followed by each of the programs in Part 2.

Chapter 1

Introduction

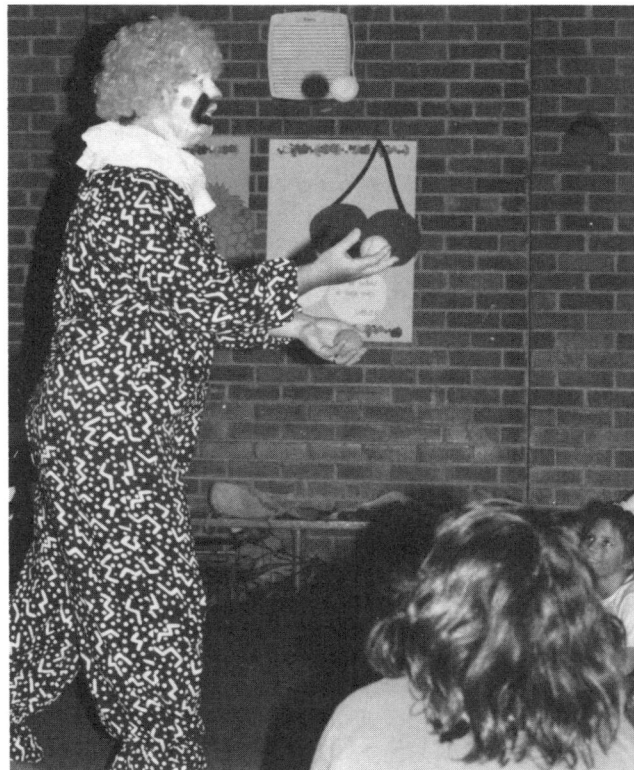

You are now a church children's club leader. Congratulations on your appointment, and welcome to the ranks of leaders who have found satisfaction and joy in this form of Christian witness and service.

If, however, you are like many others, you are experiencing your share of fear and trembling. 'What do I have to do?' 'Who will tell me how to start?' This set of learning programs has been designed to answer some of those questions. They will help you 'learn to do the job while doing it!' But before giving you some specific guidelines to help you use these learning programs to advantage, let us suggest some of the essential attributes of a church children's club leader.

What does the church, the community of faith, look for in those it entrusts to lead children? If we made a list of the qualities children's leaders should possess, it would contain many of these items. These are qualities the church prizes and values; and which it commends and desires in its children's workers.

QUALITIES PRIZED BY THE COMMUNITY OF FAITH

Children's leaders in the church can be described in these terms:

- they exhibit a strong, active Christian faith
- they display empathy; they like children and can 'tune-in' to them, and children like them
- they display leadership qualities, and show ability as effective communicators
- they are 'people-persons' and adopt a team approach
- they listen patiently to others; are consistent in their attitudes, not easily provoked, not flappable, and display patience and stickability

- they see the need for and can exercise discipline
- they are willing to train others, and be trained themselves
- they relate well to parents, and parents trust them
- they have the ability and standing to relate to the councils of the church
- and, importantly, they are people who are open to sense God's call, and to accept the work of church children's club leadership as a call of the Lord.

'But who said I had all those qualities and abilities?' You can be assured that the councils of the church have seen more than glimpses of these features in you, otherwise they would not have approached you. As you consider the work of being a children's club leader, however, keep in mind the qualities which the church prizes. These are qualitites which will grow and develop as you let your life be shaped by Jesus Christ, and as you learn and apply the skills of leadership in the children's club.

GUIDELINES FOR USING THESE LEARNING PROGRAMS

There are five learning programs in this series. Each of them has been designed to help you take practical, action steps in your club. The programs have in mind the club leader who is beginning to build experience in leadership. Here are several points to help you undertake the programs to your advantage.

CHOOSING A MENTOR

The learning programs will suggest often that you confer with a mentor, or you ask your mentor to observe the club in action. Who is a mentor?

A mentor is a friend, an acquaintance, a teacher, a minister, an elder, or indeed a spouse whom you ask to help you in your learning programs. The person does not need to be an expert in children's work.

The mentor simply needs to be one who could give you feedback, and from whom you would be prepared to receive feedback. He or she needs to be able to visit the club when you ask in order to observe the club in action as you put into practice elements of the learning programs. She or he would help you in conversation as you score your self-assessment sheets so that you can gauge your progress and assess the standards of your practice. Your mentor will be an 'outside set of eyes', a 'sounding-board', an 'observer' and an 'aide-in-learning'.

The mentor is a person of your choice:

- whose observations you will respect
- whose feedback you can trust
- who will help you think through and apply principles of club leadership in a practical manner in your club
- on the occasions, and for the topics suggested in the learning programs, and when requested by you.

Have you someone in mind to ask? Of course, it will be a personal encouragement to you if your mentor shares a Christian concern for children, is sympathetic to the work of the church, and also is one who will encourage high standards in children's work. Wherever you are, seek out a mentor. With the mentor's help, you will gain more from your participation in this series of learning programs.

When you ask your prospective mentor, give him/her time to read 'Open letter to mentors' (found in Chapter 11). As well, tell your mentor of the learning program which you want to work on first.

FEATURES OF THE LEARNING PROGRAMS

There are some features of these learning programs which make them different from other resource materials. Such features are:

1. The programs do not accentuate learning knowledge or theory, but rather stress the application of knowledge or theory in practical steps. The programs want to help you 'do the task of club leadership'.

2. The programs are self-directed. That means you decide how quickly you want to proceed and in what order you will do the programs.

3. The programs are self-paced. There is no set time in which they should be completed. You set the pace.

4. The learning place is your club. That is where you try out the steps, and where you discover what works for you and what does not. This is learning about club leadership where you are at home, even though becoming a leader is a little 'scary'. There will be other training workshops which you can attend. Take every

opportunity. In this program, however, everything is to happen in your territory.

5. This program asks you to select a mentor because the program segments call for you to discuss, to solve problems, to investigate, to design materials, to take practical steps; your mentor provides the eyes and ears you need to check your achievements.

6. These learning programs use self-assessment sheets. These give you, and the mentor, a means of checking what is or what is not happening in the club. The items on the self-assessment sheets are all about observable leader actions. This becomes a means for you to ask yourself, and your mentor, 'How well am I doing?'

7. These learning programs set performance standards, that is they recognise that leaders can learn to do the job, and then improve their skills and abilities with practice and growth in understanding. Especially in the self-assessment sheets we can recognise standards to aim for in our execution of club leadership. Is this something to be nervous about? No. It is simply a way of saying that high skill only comes through learning, experience, constructive feedback, and recognition of a standard for which to aim. If we are to lead a church children's club, then we should do it well.

In summary, the approach of these learning programs is to invite the club leader to become the key figure in a 'learning triangle'. The participants are the club leader, the mentor, and the learning program.

But what are the purposes of a children's club? Why does our church want to have a club? These are good questions to consider.

THE PURPOSE OF THE CHURCH CHILDREN'S CLUB

Here are eight purposes which answer the questions.

1. In the children's club, the claims of Jesus as Lord are to be proclaimed, and the gospel is to be expressed. Leaders will bear witness to the Lordship of Jesus Christ in their lives.

2. In the children's club, there will be a life-expanding program, related to the interests and capacities of 8–12 year old children, which will help them develop physically,

mentally, socially, morally and spiritually.

3. The children's club will provide a means for social development, particularly in developing independence and learning leadership skills.

4. The children's club will provide a training ground in prayer and Bible use, and will stimulate faith development.

5. The children's club will stimulate friendships between children and children, and children and adults, particularly creating linkages between the children and the members of the community of faith.

6. The children's club will serve as an entry point to the congregation, both for children and their families.

7. The children's club will provide means for children to interact with children and adults of the wider church.

8. The children's club will provide ways for children to experience and practise the caring work of the gospel, as children learn and serve in the neighbourhood, and for missions at home and abroad.

These are robust purposes. Such are the challenges of church children's club leadership.

The charter certificate of K.U.C.A. (Kids of the Uniting Church in Australia)[1] stipulates five points that summarise aptly the reasons why a congregation establishes a children's club. The five statements are:

1. To challenge children to accept Jesus Christ as their friend and Saviour and to nurture them in their growing relationship with him.

2. To encourage children and their families to become a part of God's family within their local church.

3. To assist children to attain a wholeness of life by sharing in spiritual, physical, social and intellectual experiences.

4. To provide an opportunity for children to serve within the church and the community.

5. To provide a means of outreach to all children.

USING THIS BOOK

The next three chapters give you material to read at any point in your learning program. Refer back to them frequently, as they remind us that our work is to reflect Jesus' ministry with children. These chapters describe the principles which are the foundations of our children's work. Then there are the five learning programs under these headings. Remember you may tackle them in any order. Begin with the one which is most pressing for you.

- Administration of a children's club
- Conducting children's club programs
- Pastoral care and faith development in a children's club
- Outreach — the children's club reaching out
- Leadership and team-building in a children's club.

To the end that children may know Jesus Christ as friend and Saviour, may grow in his likeness, and may find life in its fullness we undertake these learning endeavours.

Note

1. Official Member Charter Certificate, Kids of the Uniting Church in Australia, from Synod Office, South Australia.

Chapter 2

Jesus and his nurturing community

Of all the possible starting places for learning how to conduct a church children's club there is one central point. Jesus is our model. His regard for children was clear. It becomes obvious to us as we explore the gospel record. It also becomes clear from the New Testament that Jesus' people developed a church community which nurtured young and old in Christian living. We explore these ideas in this chapter.

JESUS' REGARD FOR CHILDREN

There are several episodes recorded in the gospels which describe sayings of Jesus concerning children. Some Christians have sentimentalised these sayings, overlaying them with views of childhood innocence. When Jesus spoke of children he was also teaching about the kingdom of God. Thus there are other complex

and demanding meanings to be reckoned with. Let us identify what Jesus showed us of his regard for children through what he said and did.

Jesus was a keen observer of children. We note this from his saying, 'To what, then, shall I compare the people of this generation, and what are they like? They are like children sitting in the market place and calling to one another, "We piped to you, and you did not dance; we wailed, and you did not weep" ' (Luke 7:31, 32). Jesus went on to point out to 'this generation' their quickness to judge the messengers of God and their blindness preventing them seeing God's presence amongst them. Jesus was criticising partial perceptions of God's presence, and the inability of the generation to recognise that his presence meant a decisive turning point in history. The teaching foreshadowed the great struggle that would culminate in the cross.

Behind this prophetic word of Jesus, using the

13

illustration of children playing at celebrations and funerals, lies his keen observation of children and their games. The insight may have come from remembrance of his own childhood games, or from spending time watching children at play. Jesus' use of 'the child' in his teachings could only have occurred because of his close and extended presence in communities where children lived and where he watched them and mingled with them at close hand.

The regard which Jesus displayed toward children becomes particularly clear when we note his actions as he taught. The disciples came to Jesus asking who is the greatest in the kingdom of heaven. 'Truly, I say to you, unless you turn and become like children, you will never enter the kindom of heaven' (Matthew 18:2–4). Jesus called the child. Jesus put the child in the midst of them. The actions in themselves had theatrical power. The child was an actual child. Jesus' attention was demonstrated. He took children in his arms. Jesus uttered the word of God by what he did. The word he demonstrated he also declared. 'Whoever humbles himself like this child, he is the greatest in the kingdom of heaven. Whoever receives one such child in my name receives me' (Matthew 18:4–5).

Further we recall the episode when parents were bringing children to Jesus and 'the disciples rebuked them. But when Jesus saw it he was indignant, and said to them: ''Let the children come to me, do not hinder them, for to such belong the kingdom of God'' ' (Mark 10:13–15). Parents wanted their children to come to Jesus. They wanted Jesus to touch them. Once again Jesus demonstrated his regard for children, in this case rebuking the disciples for their forbidding actions. Jesus clearly showed his desire for children to come. 'Do not hinder them.' And again, 'And he took them in his arms and blessed them, laying his hands upon them' (Mark 10:16).

By placing 'the child in the midst of them' Jesus clearly identified himself with children (Mathew 18:1–5; Mark 9:33–37; Luke 9:46–48). By rebuking the disciples and encouraging parents to bring their children, Jesus demonstrated his regard for children and his affinity with them. Parents and children trusted him. Children were happy to be with him. While Jesus was teaching the disciples about the nature of the kingdom, and how we are to live in the kingdom, he showed that he knew and loved children. True greatness is about becoming like a child. A child offers trust and love, which it

needs in return. The child needs care and nurture. The child became a metaphor for the disciples, or for special groups, or for the needy ones of little faith, but there can be no denying that Jesus' observations, actions and words gave high place to children.

Hans-Reudi Weber underlines significant insight from Jesus' actions. First, Jesus commends the children to our loving care. The people of God are to be hospitable to children. Second, Jesus has a special relationship to children; they are his special representatives. Third, children are the representatives of God. As such says Weber, 'they are our teachers. In their objective humility and need, they say ''mother'', ''father'', ''Abba'' and they stretch out their empty hands. If we want to learn how to become God's representatives we must learn it from the child in our midst'.[1]

When Jesus said 'Whoever receives one such child in my name receives me', he spoke to the church as it assesses its ministry. He spoke to those searching for their gifts and their personal ministry. There may be many ministries in the church and the world to be undertaken, but ministry to children is to be highly regarded because it is so close to the heart of our Lord and to the special regard he demonstrated for children.

Jesus invited us to childlike acceptance and participation in the kingdom of God. Accepting the kingdom requires both our loving trust and our recognition of our need to grow and to be reformed into the likeness of our Lord. From Jesus' regard for children we turn to the scriptural invitations to be people who grow and keep on growing toward Christian maturity.

CHRISTIAN GROWTH TOWARD MATURITY

It may seem paradoxical. Childlike trust and openness toward God are the continuing marks of the disciple. But childish faith must give way to mature faith. The Christian in openness to God is to grow toward maturity of faith. Paul made the point in his teaching that there are appropriate ways for the child to think, but which are outgrown as development occurs. 'When I was a child, I spoke like a child, I thought like a child, I reasoned like a child; when I became a man, I gave up childish ways' (1 Corinthians 13:11). Life brings experience, and broadening of understanding. That is what growing-up means.

Paul, however, clearly recognised that people

need 'to grow up in Christ.' In speaking to adults at Corinth he did not hesitate to call them 'babes in Christ'. 'But I, brothers and sisters, could not address you as spiritual people, but as people of the flesh, as babes in Christ. I fed you with milk, not solid food; for you were not ready for it; and even yet you are not ready, for you are still of the flesh' (1 Corinthians 3:1–3). There are three points to draw from Paul's picture language. The first is that we can grow in the faith, from faith-infancy to faith-maturity. Second, that the maturity of faith is not necessarily closely related to age. And the third, that whether we are mature or immature in the faith, we need to be fed, and fed with an appropriate diet.

A theme of the epistles is that the Christian life is one of continuous growth. 'Go on growing in the grace and in the knowledge of our Lord and Saviour Jesus Christ' (2 Peter 3:18). The Christian life has an objective. Elsewhere, it is described as attaining 'to the unity of the faith and of the knowledge of the Son of God, to maturity, to the measure of the stature of the fullness of Christ' (Ephesians 4:13). The Christian is to put off the old nature, and 'put on the new nature, which is being renewed in knowledge after the image of its creator' (Colossians 3:10).

To pursue Christian maturity is a lifelong task. 'Not that I have already obtained this or am already perfect; but I press on to make it my own, because Christ Jesus has made me his own' (Philippians 3:12).

The letter to the Ephesians, already mentioned, is clear about growth toward Christian maturity. The key passage is Ephesians 4:11–16, and several specific teachings can be highlighted.

How can maturity be measured? The author describes a negative and a positive measure. The negative measure is likened to childishness. 'So that we may no longer be children, tossed to and fro and carried about with every wind of doctrine, by the cunning of people, by their craftiness in deceitful wiles' (Ephesians 4:14). A maturing Christian moves away from childishness in the faith and its instability, toward Christlikeness. Positively, growth toward Christian maturity can be measured by a person's willingness to live 'speaking the truth in love' (Ephesians 4:15). Love is the key, even as Jesus commanded.

Mature personhood has three features. First it attains 'to the unity of the faith'. Maturity develops through sharing, relating and embracing the faith in the church family, the community of faith. Second, it is centred on increasing 'knowledge of the Son of God' through a continuing and deepening encounter with the Lord Jesus himself as one comes to know him more and more. Maturity develops by following obediently in discipleship and in loving relationship with Jesus Christ. Third, maturity's measure is 'the stature of the fullness of Christ'. As Ray C. Stedman explained: 'The supreme thing, the paramount thing, the thing God is after above everything else is to produce in this present world men and women who are like the humanity of Jesus Christ'.[2]

There are three other aspects to note about Christian maturity in this passage. First the Spirit gives gifts 'for the equipment of the saints, for the work of ministry, for building up the body of Christ' (Ephesians 4:12). As people discover and exercise their gifts in the body, the church, they enable others and themselves to grow. There is mutality in ministry to each other. Second, some have the gifts of apostles, prophets, evangelists, pastors and teachers. Others have gifts which are decribed in several letters. The purpose of the gifts is of a corporate nature which is building up the body of Christ and 'persons to maturity' in Jesus Christ. Gifts are given for the ultimate benefit of all. Third, Christ is the head of the body 'from whom the whole body, joined and knit together by every joint with which it is supplied, when each part is working properly, makes bodily growth and upbuilds itself in love' (Ephesians 4:16). It is not possible to understand the development of Christian maturity outside the body of Christ. The very life of the Christian community is to be the learning place which leads people on from childishness to maturity in faith and love, to the point of Christlikeness.

The ministry of fostering growth toward maturity and Christlikeness extends to all those who are of the community of faith. Its children too are to be given the appropriate encourage-ment and spiritual nourishment that will take them toward fullness in Christ. To foster growth toward Christian maturity, Christlikeness, we must recognise the place of a key factor — nurture.

NURTURE: BIBLICAL INSIGHTS

'Christian nurture is offered by Christians to Christians in order to strengthen Christian faith and to develop Christian character.'[3]

A nurturing congregation is one that shapes its life, program and relationships so that it fosters the development towards Christian maturity of its children and adults. As the letter to the Ephesians indicated, nurture is a function of the community or body of Christ. What does a congregation do to be a nurturing community?

There are insights and approaches that were known to the early church from Old Testament roots. We remember that the Christian's concern is to find out how children and adults may be nurtured so that they 'attain to the unity of the faith, and of the knowledge of the Son of God, to maturity'.

THE OLD TESTAMENT HERITAGE

In the view of Lawrence Richards, the genius of the Deuteronomy passage concerning the Mosaic practice of nurture in the home is its emphasis on participation and learning from experience of God's Word. 'Hear, O Israel: the Lord your God is one Lord; and you shall love the Lord your God with all your heart, and with all your soul, and with all your might. And these words which I command you this day shall be on your heart; and you shall teach them diligently to your children and you shall talk of them when you sit in your house, and when you walk by the way, and when you lie down, and when your rise' (Deutronomy 6:4–7). As Richards says, 'teaching God's Word was to take place in the gettings up and lyings down and walkings along the way of family life'.[4] The home and family was the important place for the learning and interpretation of God's Word and for deepening their consciousness of their place as a people in sacred history.

God's history and their history were rehearsed in home rituals 'You were brought up out of the land of Egypt' remained a constant reminder of God's plans for his people. To this day the celebration of the Passover in the Jewish home is a family ritual that involves all present. The youngest child asks the father the four questions, the first being 'Why is this night different from all other nights?'[5] Here was the nurturing practice of sacred ritual combined with family life. The practice of telling the stories and recounting their meanings was an obligation laid upon the adults, as stated in the words of the Psalmist:

We will not hide them from their children,
but tell to the coming generation
the glorious deeds of the Lord, and his might,
and the wonders which he has wrought
(Psalm 78:4).

NEW TESTAMENT PRACTICES

In the New Testament, it is not clear precisely what place children were accorded in the life of the church. Children are mentioned as Paul leaves Tyre in Acts, '. . . and they all, with wives and children, brought us on our way till we were outside the city; and kneeling down on the beach we prayed and bade one another farewell' (Acts 21:5). Neither is it clear whether children were specifically instructed as Christians, in the home or elsewhere.

We do know that the behaviour of a candidate's children was to be considered before the appointment of an elder. There are admonitions to Christian parents about the care and treatment of their children. Because homes were frequently used meeting places for the church, it is highly likely that children would have been present. Meal times and the activities of singing, praise and prayers would have been attended by children of the household. These are signs that children were participants in the Christian community.

What the New Testament does show us with some clarity was that many of the congregations were well developed in their community life. In a hostile world there was a highly developed Christian consciousness and strong relational practices. To say this is not to deny the waywardness which developed in some situations, such as at Corinth.

Church was fellowship. Early church congregations created a nurturing relational community. And if a community of faith was devoted to Christ and committed to living by his law of love, would it not have regarded its children with much care and affection? Further, if a Christian community shared such values as those frequently mentioned in the epistles (the fruits of the Spirit, for example) then that community would have yearned for the development of its members, no matter what their age. For that which helps Christians grow to maturity is that which nurtures faith in the fellowship.

Scriptures gives consistent testimony to that community's attitude towards persons. In the body of Christ individuals are valued, and this value is acted out in many ways. We have freedom to differ, and yet be accepted. We are equal with others in an ultimate sense. Each of us is spiritually significant, with a contribution to make to others. In our fellowhsip, love is more important than role. Material needs are the concern of all. In this community transparency is possible, and those who fall never fear rejection. There is forgiveness for failure, discipline when needed, and the constant affirmation of the community, for all are confident that God will enable the stumbler to grow toward Christlike maturity.[6]

What were the activities of those nurturing communities? They met together. They encouraged each other. They knew a sharing fellowship. They prayed together, and sang psalms and spiritual songs. They broke bread. They told and retold the stories of Jesus. They discussed and debated what should be the Christian rule. They treasured letters received from their Christian apostles. They contributed to the sharing of goods. They sent off funds to the needy Christians in Jerusalem. They were open to newcomers. They gave new status to women, slaves and outcasts. They rejoiced in the Spirit, discovering his gifts. And they upheld their families. It is possible that brother and sister, family terms, were adopted in the extended family of the Christian community as the most appropriate greeting for the Christian fellowship.

Communities of faith with such self perceptions and practices create a rich social and religious order which has a nurturing impact on all its members, and particularly its younger members. The congregations of the early church achieved strong nurturing fellowships. They were vigourous communities of faith that were successful in a pagan world in growing, developing and nurturing their children and newcomers. The concern for Christlike maturity and a relational community which fosters faith development in its members in experiential and participatory ways is the best setting one can imagine for the nurture of children.

We need now to consider the term 'ministry to children'. What does it mean to have a ministry? Is it meaningful to speak of ministry to children?

THE CONCEPT OF MINISTRY

Jesus' words to the disciples were: 'Even as the Son of man came not to be served but to serve, and to give his life a ransom for many' (Matthew 20:28). This is the very essence of ministry: unselfish, self-giving service in God's cause. The Christian undertaking a ministry is doing so in order to serve Christ and to serve his cause and his people. To minister in Christ's name is to do for people and communities what God

commands, and what we know 'in Christ' is necessary and good.

It is helpful to recall the *Basis of Union* of the Uniting Church in Australia for its insights on ministry.

The Uniting Church affirms that every member of the Church is engaged to confess the faith of Christ crucified and to be his faithful servant. She acknowledges with thanksgiving that the one Spirit has endowed the members of his Church with a diversity of gifts, and that there is no gift without its corresponding service: all ministries have a part in the ministry of Christ.[7]

The ministry of the Church is both a corporate and an individual ministry; to minister to the world with the ministry received from Christ (see John 13:15–17). Each must do his/her part in the whole ministry, as the metaphors of the body, or the vine suggest.

Ian Tanner proposes eight principles of ministry in the Uniting Church in Australia.

1. There is only one ministry — that of Jesus Christ.
2. Our participation in Christ's ministry is the sole purpose and glory of the Church.
3. Every member of the Church is called to participate in this one ministry.
4. Every ministry implies a prior call and gift.
5. There are varieties of ministry, but all are of equal status.
6. Leader, or equipping ministries are necessary to facilitate the every member ministry.
7. Our various ministries must be co-operative and interdependent — we are members of one body.
8. The ministry of Christ in which we share is a ministry to the whole world.[8]

A person who is called to work with children in the community of faith has a ministry in Christ's name. The regard Jesus had for children was such that we are assured of his continuing welcome to children. The purpose of this ministry is to serve children and their development toward Christian maturity and to reinforce every means for Christian nurture in the community of faith.

The ministry to children is to be shared and linked with other ministries of the congregation. Ministry to children is linked with ministries to families, young people, Christian education and at the centre the ministry of worship and fellowship.

To run a children's club to keep children off the streets may be a public service. To conduct a children's club with the purpose of nurturing and developing children toward Christian maturity, in Christ's name, is to conduct a ministry. A ministry is a shared and high calling, no matter how lowly the work may appear to be. A ministry is in the name of Christ, for Christ's purposes, and in Christ's attitude of service and care. Work so undertaken with and for children with these concerns and purposes in mind is indeed a ministry to and for children.

We have examined biblical backgrounds in regard to Jesus' attitudes towards children, examined concepts of growth and Christian maturity and aspects of the nurturing process, and finally noted the concept of ministry. Now let us draw these together for the children's club leader in terms of principles to guide action.

PRINCIPLES FOR THE CHILDREN'S CLUB LEADER

We serve Christ when we serve children in Christ's name. We recall how Jesus observed, attended to and blessed children. He enjoyed rapport with them. He called for their presence. He was an advocate for children when the disciples attempted to turn them away. His actions declared his regard for them. Jesus used childlikeness as a symbol of the trust needed to accept the kingdom. Jesus commended children children to our care. We are to see them as God's representatives amongst us.

As church children's club leaders we participate in the ministry of growth and development of children towards Christian maturity and Christlikeness. The goal for Christians is to grow into Christlikeness and to demonstrate in life the qualities of Christ. This is to be achieved in a community of believers where members exercise their gifts and share mutual ministry for their equipping as Christians. Children and adults participate in developing Christlikeness.

A community that shapes its life and work on the achievement of Christlikeness and nurtures its children and adults to live by Christian care and commitment will serve Christ's cause. Children are to be nurtured toward Christian maturity. The New Testament provides us with examples and teachings of relational community life that nurtures members towards Christlikeness. A community that cares, loves, forgives, affirms and supports its people,

pivoting its fellowship on Christ, is a nurturing community. To serve children in that style of nurturing community is a people-building and maturity enhancing ministry towards 'the fullness of the stature of Christ'.

Ministry among children is a ministry shared with the whole ministry of Christ. Work among children is ministry when given in Christ's name, for Christ's cause, for the establishment of children's relationships to Christ and his church.

These are biblical and theological principles which will guide a children's club leader's active ministry to children. There are further issues to be considered especially as we focus on the child between eight and twelve years of age. These are the developmental principles to which we turn in the next chapter.

Notes

1. Hans-Reudi Weber, *Jesus and the Children*, John Knox Press, Atlanta, 1979, p. 51.
2. *Body Life* by Ray C. Steadman. © Copyright 1972, Regal Books, Ventura CA 93006. Used by permission. The extract is on page 24.
3. British Council of Churches Consultative Group on Ministry among Children, *The Child in the Church*, British Council of Churches, 1984, p.51.
4. Taken from *A Theology of Children's Ministry* retitled in 1988 *Children's Ministry* by Lawrence O. Richards. Copyright © 1983 by The Zondervan Corporation. This extract is on p. 250.
5. Stewart Dicks, Paul Mennill and Donal Santor, *The Many Faces of Religion: an enquiry approach*, Ginn and Company, Canada, 1973, p. 171.
6. Richards, p.43.
7. The Assembly Standing Committee of the Uniting Church in Australia, *Constitution and Regulations and The Basis of Union*, (The Joint Board of Christian Education — Uniting Church Press, Melbourne, revised 1984), pa. 13, p. 10.
8. Ian B. Tanner, *A Handbook for Elders*, Uniting Church Press, Melbourne, 1984, p. 13.

Chapter 3

Children as developing learners

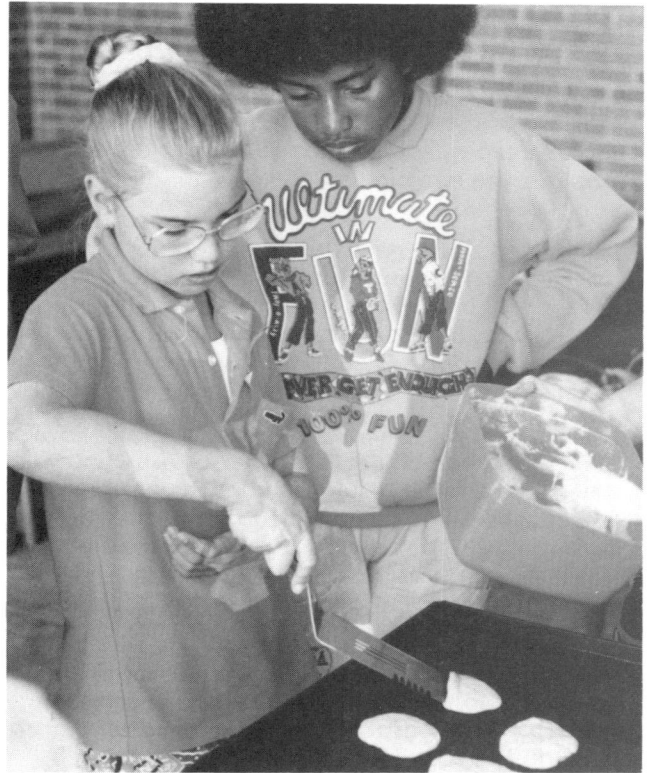

Shape them as though they are statues was John Chrysostom's word to parents (c. 347–407 AD).

> Like the creators of statues do you give all your leisure to fashioning these wondrous statues for God. And, as you remove what is superfluous and add what is lacking, inspect them day by day, to see what good qualities nature has supplied so that you will increase them, and what faults so that you will eradicate them.[1]

Are children like pieces of wax or marble to be carved into shape by an adult sculptor? Certainly not! We know that children have minds of their own. We know too, that the environment in which the child lives will influence its growth. Such factors as the impressions made by people and the interactions between the child, other children and adults are significant. Likewise a person's inner drives for growth, require us to recognise that the child is active in the process of its own mental, moral and spiritual growth. It is vital to our understanding that we recognise that children are developing learners.

This chapter will help us clarify how much or how little we should expect of the eight to twelve year old child. The content of programs, the methods of Bible exploration, the types of stories and the depth of discussions we employ may all be influenced by our understandings of the ability of children to cope.

Our first step in describing children as developing learners is to see that children change in their manner or style of thinking as they develop.

CHILDREN'S CHANGING PATTERNS OF THOUGHT[2]

Here are the stories of John and Henry. Children of different ages are likely to bring different responses to questions about the two episodes. Consider the two stories.

John is in his room when his mother calls him to dinner. John goes down and opens the door to the dining room. But behind the door is a chair, and on the chair is a tray with fifteen cups on it. John does not know the cups are behind the door. He opens the door, the door hits the tray, bang go the fifteen cups, and they all get broken.

One day when Henry's mother is out, Henry tries to get some biscuits out of the cupboard. He climbs up on a chair, but the biscuit jar is still too high, he cannot reach it. He had been told not to touch the biscuit jar. While trying to reach the jar, he knocks over a cup. The cup falls down and breaks.[3]

Who was the naughtiest? A five year old is likely to say that John was the naughtiest because he broke the large number of cups. An eight year old is likely to say Henry was the naughtiest because he disobeyed an instruction. John was being obedient, but had an accident. Henry was disobedient doing something he was instructed not to do.

Why this difference in viewpoint? The older child has developed the capacity to understand the difference between obedience and disobedience on the one hand, and damage because of accident and damage because of wrong intention on the other. The older child is not swayed by the number of cups broken, whereas the younger child will be persuaded by the amount of damage caused.

The change is explained by the increased capacity of the older child to think in a more mature and comprehensive style. Several more years of life have given him a thinking capacity to understand and interpret more comprehensively. The child has been restructuring his understandings and enlarging mental horizons as he actively attempts to make sense of the world round about.

What are the features of this process of the changing patterns and styles of thinking? Three comments can be made.

First, there are signs which show that people are using different patterns of thinking. The ability to see the difference between intentional disobedience and obedience is not present in the younger child, but can be in an older child. The ability to deal with concepts such as 'atonement', 'redemption', 'human rights' or 'equal opportunity' will not come until the mental structures are ready, perhaps in later adolescence.

The children of children's club age are likely to be concrete thinkers. That is, they will use methods of thinking which are story-like. If they are thinking about 'school' it will be as a place, a room, a class, a teacher, and the activities and games of the playground. They will not think in terms of concepts of education, discipline, or student-teacher relationships. They are not yet ready for such conceptual thinking. Their pattern is as 'concrete thinkers'.

Second, new patterns of thinking are stimulated by interactions. Moving towards more mature patterns comes about through several forces acting on the child. There is on the one hand the child thinking for herself, but on the other there is the life setting. The child is confronted by many people of many types and ranges, and many situations all of which prompt the mind to be busy coping with various impressions.

Some situations will encourage more comprehensive thinking, especially when the child is asked to solve problems or be engaged in projects.

Third, having a 'quizzical' or 'unsettled' mind is a feature of developing new patterns of thinking. New ways of thinking challenge the mind, but unsettle it, and we look for a new way to put all the ideas, old and new, together. This is a normal human process. Eventually — though the experience is unsettling — we learn how to resolve the ideas and our mental ability has grown and we perhaps have developed a more mature or comprehensive pattern of thought. The process of reasoning development is by stimulation, then feeling out of balance, then shaping a new structure of thinking that draws it all together into a new balance. Such is the process through which children are moving as they develop more and more mature patterns of thought.

These same insights apply in regard to how children use their reasoning when deciding on what is right or wrong. Moral judgment also develops.

CHILDREN THINKING ABOUT WHAT IS RIGHT

There are changing patterns of moral thinking. Once again, we need to see children as developing learners. Here are the answers of children who were asked the question, 'How do you know what is right or wrong to do?'

Gillian, 7:
If Mum or a teacher tells you what to do you do it, but if someone tells you not to do that you don't do it.

Conrad, 8:
If someone is cross with you, you don't do that thing again.

Adam, 8:
At home and school I am told if it is right or wrong.

Joan, 11:
If I have been told it's wrong and I do it I get a bad feeling. Most of the time I go along with other people in what they do.

John, 13:
I think it is wrong when you hurt someone's feelings or do something they don't like.

Durk, 16:
Your conscience tells you whether something is right or wrong. This is based on what you have learnt, public opinion, your friends' ideas and so on.

Emma, 16:
One must use one's own judgment in these things, remembering the influences of your parents and friends and having regard for the law and rules of the game.

Big changes in styles of thinking occur through the childhood and adolescent years, especially in stimulating environments. The younger children make their decisions on whether they will be punished or not, or on what authorities have told them, whilst older children like Joan and John are beginning to consider others. They are now seeing the need to both be concerned about others feelings as well as gaining approval from others.The adolescents, Durk and Emma, realise they must use their own judgment in making up their minds.

These are different patterns or stages of thinking about moral matters. They signify how growing up and life experience result in developing more comprehensive patterns of thinking. These are clues to what it means for children to be seen as developing learners.

It will be useful to draw a word picture of children of club age. Where are they coming from? What are they now? What lies ahead? The following is a sketch. It is generalised. It may not fit particular children or every situation. Broadly, however, it reminds us of the limitations of children which enthusiastic adults may overlook.

CLUB AGED CHILDREN — WHERE ARE THEY COMING FROM?

Children in the church club are coming from the magical years. God, nature and their parents were treated in rather magical terms. Their verbal and conceptual ability has not developed. Imitation of people and situations has been a major approach in their learning. Their play has had a serious purpose for that is how they have interpreted and reconstructed the world for themselves. Their view has been egocentric. They have not been able to understand that another could have a view or need any different from their own. They have not been able to appreciate that when mother has influenza, she cannot be outside playing with them. Seeing another's situation has been beyond their understanding. They have not been able to explain their reasons for behaviour or their opinion. 'It just is.'

They have been assessing what is right in terms of 'what is good for me or what my parents tell me is right'. Some may have reached the point where what is right is judged by whether one is punished or rewarded because of the action. Some may be beginning to use tit-for-tat thinking as the basis for choosing what is right. This is the pattern of satisfying one's own needs by exchange.

CLUB AGE CHILDREN — WHAT ARE THEY BECOMING?

In the years 8–12, children will make many changes. They will discover cause and effect. They begin to link events. They become less egocentric. They can differentiate self from others, and they can undertake co-operative endeavours. They are curious with active imaginations. They will continue to think of God in physical terms for a while. Prayer relates to particular times and activities. Later in the period they will think of prayer as conversation with God.

They are concrete thinkers. For example, Christmas and Easter are about what the child receives. Later, these celebrations will be perceived in terms of Jesus and the church. During these years, they develop the capacities to distinguish variables, and to perceive objects, numbers, time and space. These are the years of the story. They need stories from Bible and human experience which help them remember and understand. In moral terms, there will be some who will begin to assess right or wrong in terms of approval and disapproval. Love, kindness and happiness are seen to be pleasant and approval gaining qualities. The 'good boy, nice girl' pattern begins to appear.

CLUB AGE CHILDREN — WHERE ARE THEY GOING NEXT?

The phase still lies ahead where children begin to think abstractly. The sense of history will develop. The ability to use concepts will be attained through the adolescent years when the young person is able to think about thinking. Then he or she will be able to use hypothetical and deductive reasoning, and thinking can be about propositions or principles. Some will begin to assess what is right in terms of law, order, authority and social order. The notion of society develops. Let it be said some adults do not develop to this stage.

What lessons can be drawn from this sketch? To recognise that the children of the club are 'concrete thinkers' and use patterns of reasoning about right and wrong that are appropriate for their age is to encourage leaders to pay special attention to find fitting ways of communicating with these children. Later in this segment more attention will be given to such approaches.

Having briefly surveyed development of thinking patterns, what can be said about faith development?

THE DEVELOPMENT OF FAITH

We can illustrate different patterns of faith within the pages of the New Testament.[4] To examine these will help us see different patterns of faith amongst children and young people.

There is a style of faith which seems to have 'its eye on the benefits'. We can call this *Level one* faith. James and John requested Jesus, 'Grant us to sit, one at your right hand and one at your left, in your glory'. (Mark 10:35–35). Their faith and trust in the Lord is marked by self-centred concerns. It is faith to gain pleasure or reward; and avoid punishment and fear. It reflects the idea of trusting the Lord for the benefit it will bring.

There is a style of faith which is typified by mechanical obedience; this we can call *Level two*. In Matthew 7:21–27 and Luke 6:46–49, Jesus describes levels of obedience. It may be easy to say 'Lord, Lord' and claim to be obedient, but true obedience is exercised by those who do the will of the Father. *Level two* faith is that which says 'I want to please him, for he is my Lord. I will obey him. I will do what he says'.

Trust describes *Level three* faith. This faith level is based on trust and a personal relationship. 'Abide in me and I in you' (John 14:4). The attitude can be described as 'I have experienced Christ in my life. I have obeyed him. I trust him. I want to discover and share his mind'. That was the search of the rich young man who desired to follow Christ but who could not take the step of 'giving away' (Matthew 19:16–30; Luke 18:18–30).

Self-giving, relational love signifies a mature style of faith. This we can call *Level four* faith. Here the theme is *agape*: love which places higher regard for the other than for oneself. It is self-giving, losing oneself in unquestioning, totally giving *agape* (Luke 10:25–27; Mark 12:28–34). Its expression is 'I can do no other; he has my heart, my mind, my soul. I am his and he is mine'.

It is possible to see such different styles of faith. How can children's faith be fostered from immature to mature forms? There are two keys to nurturing faith in children as developing learners.

KEYS TO FAITH DEVELOPMENT

The first key is that the congregation is the setting of influence and stimulation for the maturing of faith.[5] Faith development is fostered by what the community of faith does to and for its members. It is a community that transmits its faith to its members by witnessing, modelling, and setting a living example. The community teaches its religious values by transmission. It creates and perpetuates a culture. Its people do what Christians do. The people, adults and children, participate in its rituals and develop in their relationships. The community of faith transmits or passes on its faith in a living way.

Thus in a community of faith that recognises that its main education and formative method is participation in Christian community, deeper value is given to essential experiences for Christians such as:

- celebrating the Christian festivals
- making strong use of the sacraments
- emphasising rites of passage
- enjoying one another and being grateful for several generations
- acting as Christians together in the name of Christ for the needy.

Faith develops by adults and children acting as a community and participating as Christians. For children in the faith community, faith is that which is experienced together in all the activities, celebrations and worship. As the child grows, a deeper desire to belong and be part of the congregation can develop — to be affliliated with the people and the procedures of the Christian community. The child enjoys involvement and interprets faith as doing what Christians do.

A more personal faith beckons. There is an inner search for meaning. Probing questions unsettle satisfaction with the previous style of affiliation. The questioning or wondering experience is a critical time for faith development. Faith does not deepen unless we wonder and explore our experience and the Christian truths. But the lack of a sympathetic environment that does not allow children and young people to question and probe for meaning can mean that some are not encouraged through this period of potential growth in faith. For those that are, there comes the experience of an 'owned' faith, where the person both owns the faith personally, and also is owned by the faith.

Christian experience has shown that mature faith has a see-saw image. We tip from 'questioning to owning' and from 'owning to questioning'. That is the rhythm of a continuing growth in faith.

That picture of growth is set within the congregation as a community of faith that intentionally enculturates its members. The community of faith which is confident in its ministry, takes Paul's word seriously, 'What you have learned and received and heard and seen in me, do; and the God of peace will be with you'. (Philippians 4:9).

The power of transmitting the Christian culture is a key factor in fostering faith development. The method is age-old; it is the way of the tribe. The view has significance for workers with children because it places so much stress on shared experience and participation. It trusts relationships and experiences built around the central acts of Christian worship, fellowship and action to foster the development of faith.

The second key in understanding faith development in children is to recognise the human desire to find values to trust and live by. James Fowler calls this process 'faithing'.[6] 'Faithing' is the active search for faith.

'Faithing' can be explained in this way. It is a human search to desire and discover ideals to live by. We do not always know what our search means, or indeed that we are searching. How am I going to shape my life? What will I believe in? What ideals will I trust? Who are the ones with values worth accepting? We begin to locate and define ideals worth trusting through the relationships we develop. Our self identity and our centres of power and value and the objects of our trust and loyalty result from our internal questionings and considerations of the lives around us.[7]

The faithing search can be represented by a triangle, involving self, others, and worthy values, ideals or centres of power which can be trusted. (Fig. 1)

Shared centres of value and power

Figure 1

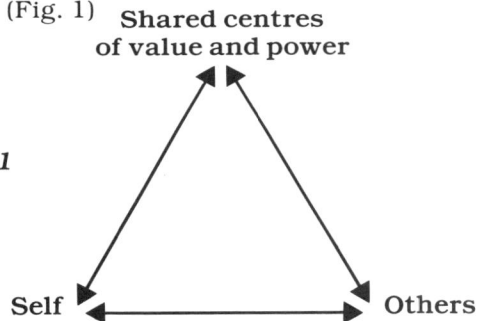

Self   **Others**

We find the ideals to trust, our faith, in relationships as we discover what others trust in the faith they hold. It is a relational search. The relationships are vertical as well as horizontal. The person is active in the process as we seek the faith to hold.

The key area of 'faithing' reminds us that children are active in their own development. Developing a faith is not something that adults do to children. Children are not empty mugs to be filled from the adult faith jug. Rather, children are observing, listening, puzzling, experimenting and shaping the faith values that have meaning for them from their encounters in human experience. Adults who are continuing to grow in faith follow a similar search.

These, then, are two keys to faith development:

1. faith develops in us, and in our children, as we participate in the life of the community of faith

2. faith develops in us through our own searching, discovering and restructuring processes as through interactions and relationships we find the ideals to live by.

In the Christian community, one key supports the other. A nurturing congregation witnesses the lordship and friendship of Jesus Christ, one to the other. The nurturing congregation recognises that individuals are searching for meaning. It fosters and encourages personal growth. Care and recognition are the signs of an educating and nurturing fellowship.

Having briefly surveyed the elements of development, we can be clearer in our understanding of the child with whom we deal in the children's club. We can summarise the characteristics of the eight to twelve year old child.

THE CHILD IN THE CHILDREN'S CLUB

The eight to twelve year old is filled with curiosity, eager for experiences, open to friendships with children of similar ages and with respected adults. These children will be concrete thinkers, not ready for abstract or theological concepts, but well able to appreciate concrete examples of 'truth in life'. There are limitations in their reasoning, moral judgment and faith positions simply because there has not been time to handle the structural shifts and changes that stimulation and age can bring.

As an example, their understanding of the Golden Rule will be related to their reasoning abilities to deal with its wisdom. Children continuing to use early styles of moral judgment will use the Golden Rule to mean 'if somebody hits you, you hit him back'. Or perhaps, 'if you are nice to people they will be nice back to you'. Children of club age may delight in memorising the Golden Rule, but their understanding of it will be related to their present reasoning abilities. The Golden Rule has such profundity that Lawrence Kohlberg, for instance, used it as an example of the most mature moral reasoning. The club child can learn it and use it, but we have to recognise that the child uses it as a concrete operator.

PRINCIPLES — FOR WORKING WITH CLUB CHILDREN WHO ARE DEVELOPING LEARNERS

In looking for principles for children's club work, this is the first. These children are concrete thinkers. As a worker with children, the club leader needs to find the ways which are relevant to concrete thinkers to stimulate their reasoning, moral judgment and faith capacities to develop further. How can the club leader offer a rich environment for children's development? How can the club leader prevent himself/herself from placing children out of their depth with church theology or doctrine? Here are some pieces of advice which come from a range of writers.

June Wright commends to club leaders the aim of giving children 'real experiences'. What does that mean? It means children doing it themselves. Meeting people. Interpreting the Bible themselves. Participating in program segments themselves and expressing their ideas.[8]

Lawrence Richards builds much of his concept of ministry to children on five processes. These, he says, influence the growth of faith, and much else besides. His five processes 'are those that:

- communicate belonging to a vital faith community
- involve participation in the life of a vital faith community
- facilitate modelling on members of the faith community
- provide biblical instruction as interpretation-of-life
- encourage growing exercise of personal choice'.[9]

We note Richards' active words: belonging, participation, modelling, interpretation-of-life, and exercise of personal choice. Modelling, in particular, we will examine in Chapter 7.

Roger and Gertrude Gobbel provide another clue in their critique of a Christian education process that tells children about the Bible and about information in it. This approach 'diverts children from the work of engaging the Bible directly as they are able'.[10] They advocate methods that allow children to be interpreters of the Bible themselves. Let children use the Bible in their way, and let the adult listen to their discoveries of meaning.

John Westerhoff[11] accentuates the participation of children in the celebrations and fellowship of the community of faith. Both Stanley Hauerwas[12] and Westerhoff accentuate the telling of the story. We are the people of the story. We tell and retell in many ways the story of God's dealing with people through history, especially through Jesus. We know who and whose we are through the story. Concrete thinkers, above all, are lovers of a story. Both the story and the stories that embrace or describe the Christian pilgrimage are the avenues to the heart of the child.

PRINCIPLES TO FOSTER DEVELOPMENT

The principles to be applied by club leaders use 'active' words. The over-riding principle is to accentuate experiences, involvement and participation. Engage children in working with the Bible, and the Christian story. Seek ways for children to make choices and decisions. Give them experience in discussion. Give them real life stories and seek children's interpretations of them. Give them opportunity to discover, and to be curious. Let them meet people and ask them questions. Let them create and dramatise and paint. Let them interpret with art and craft. Concrete thinkers need the stimulation of experiences more than they need philosophical concepts, or ideas too far advanced.

The children's club leader will recognise that the club has the potential to stimulate the development of children in all dimensions. The leader will constantly ask, 'How can I devise this program so that children are fully engaged? How can this worship, this activity, this Bible story, this craft time be framed to let children work with the matter themselves? How can I find the way for children to decide and interpret on their own terms?' The leader open to these questions will be tuned to the needs of eight to twelve year old children as they develop.

Having briefly surveyed the developmental needs of children, we turn to examine principles that a congregation needs to consider under the heading — the Club in the Context of Children's Ministry.

Notes

1. John Crysostom, quoted by Lawrence O. Richards, *A Theology of Children's Ministry*, Zondervan, Grand Rapids, 1983, p. 50.
2. Two writers have been influential in the matter of child development — Jean Piaget on cognitive development and Lawrence Kohlberg on cognitive moral reasoning. Their views, on which the points in this segments are based, can be drawn from several sources: Iris V. Cully, *Christian Child Development* (Joint Board of Christian Education, Melbourne, 1979); Ronald Duska and Mariellen Whelan, *Moral Development: A guide to Piaget and Kohlberg* (Paulist Press, New York, 1975); Peter Scharf (ed.), *Readings in Moral Education* (Winston Press, Minneapolis, 1978); Jean Piaget, *The Child's Conception of the World* (Paladin, St Albans, Herts, 1929, 1977) and *The Moral Judgment of the Child* (Middlesex: Penguin Books, 1932); and Barry J. Wadsworth, *Piaget's Theory of Cognitive Development* (David McKay Co. Inc., New York, 1971).
3. Stories adapted from Duska and Whelan, p. 115.
4. I am indebted to John Dettoni, *Ecology of Faith Development Syllabus* (Fuller Theological Seminary, Pasadena, 1985), for this outline of levels of faith.
5. The work of John Westerhoff III, has been influential in describing 'enculturing' or 'socializing' models for developing faith. John Westerhoff III, *Will our Children have faith?* Dove Communications, Melbourne, 1976.
6. James W. Fowler, *Stages of Faith: The Psychology of Human Development and the Quest for Meaning*, Dove Communications, Melbourne, 1981 pp. 91ff. See also Jim Fowler, Sam Keen and Jim Berryman (eds), *Life Maps — Conversations on the Journey of Faith*, Word Inc., Waco, Texas, 1978.
7. Fowler, p. 91ff.
8. June Wright, *When Children Meet: Church Clubs for Children 8–13*, Joint Board of Christian Education, Melbourne, 1974, p. 11.
9. Richards, p. 76.
10. Roger Gobbel and Gertrude Gobbel, *The Bible — A Child's Playground*, SCM Press, London, 1986, from the Preface, p. ix.
11. John Westerhoff, III, *Living the Faith Community: The Church that makes a difference*, Winston Press, Minneapolis, 1985, p. 25 and p. 27.
12. Stanley Hauerwas, *A Community of Character. Toward a Constructive Christian Social Ethic*, Indiana, University of Notre Dame Press, 1981, pp. 9ff.

Chapter 4

The club in the context of children's ministry

'Give high priority to children, youth and young adults.' John Bodycomb, in the 1986 Northey Lectures went on to say:

> To address the matter merely because we saw children, youth and young adults as 'pew fodder' would be immoral, of course; the issue is how they may appropriate in their own ways the benefits of life in a religious community. The issue is critical for every parish and every denomination. It undoubtedly calls for some changes which may not be without pain for the rest of us.[1]

David Merritt, Executive Director of the Joint Board of Christian Education, in the report to the 1988 Assembly of the Uniting Church in Australia, commented on ministry with children. The report stated:

> There has been a remarkable upsurge of interest all around Australia in ministry with children. Questions about how children participate in worship and how we share the faith with children raise the most fundamental issues about the nature of the gospel and the nature of the church.[2]

These are pleas for congregations to consider carefully their ministry to children and how it will be exercised. There are decisions to be made about programs and strategies which are pertinent for any congregation that is serious about children's work. There is a need to seek out church program principles in regard to ministry to children.

In this chapter, we will examine several issues briefly. First, there are many approaches or program options which a congregation may adopt as they undertake ministry to children. Several of these will be named. Second, there are specific reasons why a congregation may choose to offer ministry with children through a children's club. These reasons provide a rationale for club work. Third, we will survey the objectives for a club. We will list some of the educational strengths of the club approach and will conclude with the stated aims of the club movement — Kids of the Uniting Church in Australia. The final material will focus on the principles that a club leader will value and that will help in shaping his or her contribution to club leadership. And so we ask what choices are open to a congregation about exercising ministry to children?

CHOICES FOR THE CONGREGATION

The congregation which recognises that ministry to children must be a high priority in its total work has a number of options about how it can exercise that ministry. There is a range of options that are not necessarily exclusive. Some congregations will adopt several of these approaches. Here are some possibilities.

First, the emphasis on ministry to children could be through 'all ages together' worship. The congregation could value having three or four generations in worship together and focus on children in the process. Energy could be given to involvement of children in worship, looking for maximum participation from children, even to having children on the worship planning committee from time to time. The fellowship would be active in incorporating families, and ensuring that the children were known by name and treated as valued members of the worshipping congregation.

Second, the congregation could undertake ministry to children through Sunday school. Stress would be on recruiting teachers and departmental leaders who would accept the work as a ministry to children. Training and equipping of teachers would be prized. Outreach to children of the community would be encouraged. Sunday school events such as picnics and class activities would allow the development of relationships. Classes would be in age groups and a curriculum would be adopted or devised.

Third, the congregation could pursue ministry to children as one of the thrusts of family clusters developed to deepen the sense of community in the congregation. Activities of the families could give priority to welcoming each others children and caring for them. Parents appear to respond more readily to fellowship and mutual modelling of Christian parenthood and care for children than they do to lectures about Christian nurture and family life.

Fourth, the congregation in its ministry to children could adopt the plan of establishing its own Christian school. It could see its own property being used as the venue for a registered primary or secondary school. The board of the school would be established with a continuing membership of church people as well as parents. The congregation would accept the role of continuing involvement with the school. It could view this endeavour as its ministry to children.

Fifth, the congregation could adopt a method of concentrating on home and family life. Lawrence Richards describes a vision of this method in *A New Face for the Church* (Zondervan Publishing, Grand Rapids, 1970) in which gifted visitors become stimulators and facilitators as well as supporters of Christian nurture in families and home life.[3]

Sixth, sporting teams of various kinds for children, youth and adults (including entering teams in church competitions) could be adopted as a major thrust for ministry to children. Boys and girls teams in various sports could be recruited. Coaches, supervisors and referees would be selected from interested people in the congregation. Fellowship activities would provide a further social dimension.

Seventh, the congregation could decide on a children's club as a means for ministry to children. While there could be a club for primary children, there would be follow-on clubs for junior and senior adolescents.

These seven examples of approaches to children's work are sufficient to underscore the view that the congregation has options about its methods for ministry to children. Its decisions will be based on local needs. The congregation should not turn away from its obligation to minister to children, but it can choose the program methods that seem most relevant to their needs and their people. Some congregations will pursue their ministry to children by undertaking several of these strategies concurrently. There are two points to make after recognising the range of possible methods:

1. the conducting of a church children's club is one option for exercising ministry to children; and

2. a comprehensive ministry to children will not rely on one method only.

Each method has particular advantages and disadvantages. Where adult leadership is available or can be recruited and equipped, a congregation will be well advised to use several of these approaches in its ministry. Much can be achieved if the congregation values 'all ages together' worship that fosters a sense of Christian community. From that base energy can flow into the expression of its ministry in many directions. A church children's club can be one of these forms of ministry.

Why choose a children's club as a method for ministering to children? There are particular reasons that give strength to the case for club work in a congregation as a ministry to children.

WHY CHOOSE A CHILDREN'S CLUB?

Here are six reasons for a congregation to undertake children's club work.

1. A children's club provides a means for children of like age to be together and to extend and deepen their friendships. Many of them will be from church-going families, many will not. Many will know each other from school, although in some places the children will go to a range of schools. Friendship and peer support as young Christians is a positive feature of club life. Peer influence and involvement are vitally important for this age group of 8–12. Children tend to follow their friends. If friends are also involved in such activities as church club, then there is mutual support and encouragement. In this environment, it will be easier for them to talk, listen and contribute to Christian activity.

2. A children's club places respected and significant Christian adults in the environment where they can befriend children. Such adults give time to friendship and activity with children. They commit time to children. Thus the congregation will need to exercise care in selecting persons for club leadership. Adults who can establish rapport with children, who have a vibrant faith, who have patience and who will earnestly seek the growth of children in the Christian faith will be the type of adults required. Parents, of course, need to trust them, as well as the elders and minister. A children's club gives children significant adult friendship.

3. The children's club has the advantage of offering a weeknight activity for children, leaving Sundays for worship with an 'all ages together' thrust, and also for Sunday school.

A weeknight has several positive features. It provides an outing for children, but more importantly it allows a diverse club program to be developed, ranging from visits to visitors to knock-about games and to messy crafts.

4. The children's club approach can dovetail with other programs in the church directed towards families, especially in outreach. A club will give some parents their first contact with the congregation when their children join. The elders and ministers have a point of contact; and the children and parents have a point of entry to the church.

5. The children's club has greater flexibility than a Sunday school or sports club to emphasise several important factors necessary for children's moral and spiritual development. First is in the area of relationships — adult to child, child to child. The club can use small groups of stable membership as well as adhoc groupings for particular activities. It will use a mixed gender leadership team probably with a spread of ages. This mix will ensure that children will find somebody, if not a number, with whom they can feel close. Second, the club can provide the setting for more creative strategies for Bible exploration and expression. It can give time to art, drama and movement that would not be possible in a sports team, or even in Sunday school where there are time restrictions. Third, the club can be the setting for 'real experiences' that foster faith expansion. The club has the task of developing a meaningful program but it is not tied to a curriculum or even a classroom model of activity.

6. A club offers a particular advantage to children, from their point of view. It is specifically for children. Its program content, its methods, its forms and fun, its excitements are related to the 8–12 year old. The adults are present to facilitate and promote involvement for and by children. They are to provide a child-centred program. The club's life is age specific.

These are six reasons why a congregation may adopt the use of a children's club as a means for ministry to children. But we must consider some costs.

COSTS TO THE CONGREGATION IN FORMING A CHILDREN'S CLUB

There are some costs to a congregation in undertaking club work. These points can be mentioned.

1. The congregation needs to be able to recruit suitable adults who meet their expectations of Christian maturity, and who are also able to work creatively with children.

2. The adults chosen need to have the potential to develop programs that are creative and life-expanding for children. Programs that assist children's faith development and growth in Christian character will be marked by good understanding of the developmental ages and stages of children. The adult leaders also need a sense of freedom that will allow children to explore and engage matters of the faith at their own level.

3. The congregation may need to consider the adequacy of its property for children's club use. Are there suitable light chairs that children can move? Are there sufficient work tables? Are toilets adequate, accessible and safely placed? Are the hall entrances well lit? Is the hall floor suitable for games and activities or is it too shiny or too splintered? Will the club have access to kitchen facilities? Can the club have secure storage facilities? The congregation should take the state of its property into consideration and be prepared to count the property and equipment costs in establishing children's club work.

4. The congregation must have a commitment to the club. The most debilitating factor for a club leader is to feel forgotten by the congregation. The club cannot be fully effective in its work if it is not part of the community of faith. There need to be constant efforts to incorporate the children in the worshipping congregation. The community of faith must also affirm and support the club leader team. They must not be left to work alone. For a congregation to adopt a children's club approach to ministry to children, there is an ongoing cost or commitment to maintain support, interest and encouragement.

Congregations may hesitate on these grounds. The potential for ministry to children through a club, however, is great. Ultimately, the congregation, elders and ministers need to assess the long term potential of any of the methods, and particularly the use of children's club, in the light of its long range purpose of developing children in their Christian faith.

Let us examine the work of a children's club more closely, by means of mission statements.

THE MISSION OF A CHURCH CHILDREN'S CLUB

These eight mission statements will be useful to both the congregation and any prospective leader in considering the aims and objectives of a club.

1. The children's club will provide a context for the gospel to be expressed and for the claims of Jesus as Lord to be voiced and witnessed. Its leaders are commissioned to bear witness to the Lordship of Jesus Christ in their lives. Children as peers and as young Christians will be able to declare their faith in Christ in discussion, activities, creative expression and the worship of the club.

2. The children's club will provide a program that is related to the interests and capacities of 8–12 year old children. The program will be life-expanding. It will open up new vistas for children. Eight year old children face an incredibly fascinating world. Children's club can bring new experiences to them. This does not mean grandiose programs, but it means recognising that a young child's adventure lies in lighting a fire to cook, using a hammer and saw, meeting an entertainer, assisting an elderly person, playing games different from any encountered before, and turning the Bible into drama, dance and captivating story. It means paint, craft and creativity.

3. The children's club will provide a means for social development. For many, this will be their first 'on-their-own' regular evening outing. It will be different from other experiences, especially different from school. But learning to work with others, eating with others, and learning courtesies are elements of social development. Learning to speak in front of others in saying grace, leading in prayers, reading the Bible or giving a speech of thanks represent aspects of social education through the children's club.

4. The children's club will provide a training ground in prayer and Bible familiarity, using

methods attuned to this age group. It will stimulate faith development especially if the leaders pay close attention to engaging children's imaginations by employing a variety of involvement methods in offering prayer and using the Bible.

5. The children's club will stimulate the development of friendships between children and between children and adults. It will create links between the children and members of the community of faith so that these children will learn that they are valued by the community of faith at worship and other fellowship settings.

6. The children's club will be promoted and valued by the community of faith as an entry point to the congregation. It will reach out to children not involved in church. It will be the reason for the community of faith to come to know the families of new children. This is seen as a responsibility of the congregation and not only of the club leaders.

7. The children's club will provide opportunities for children to interact with children and adults of the wider church. This may happen through rallies, picnic days or campouts. Such experiences introduce the concept of the wider church and affirm to children that the church values and respects their presence and involvement.

8. The children's club will reinforce in practical ways the challenge of the gospel to care. By helping children to learn about and work for missions at home and abroad, the club will encourage children to adopt the outreach concerns of the congregation. They will have the voice and the ability to decide on specific projects in the life of the club.

These eight statements represent the mission objectives of a children's club. The charter certificate of K.U.C.A. (Kids of the Uniting Church in Australia) gives five succinct and essential objectives of a church children's club. These are:

1. To invite children to trust Jesus Christ as their Saviour and Friend.

2. To enourage children and their families to become part of God's family within their local church.

3. To assist children to attain a wholeness of life by sharing in spiritual, physical, social and intellectual experiences.

4. To provide an opportunity for children to serve within the church and the community.

5. To provide a means of outreach to all children.[4]

CHURCH PROGRAM PRINCIPLES

I have explained that the local congregation has a number of options open to it about the methods it may choose to use in the exercise of ministry to children. If it is able, the congregation may decide to use several of these options. They are not mutually exclusive.

To decide to use a children's club is a deliberate step by the congregation, being aware of the particular advantages of club ministry and of the costs it will demand in leader recruitment and ongoing congregational support.

It is a deliberate step, knowing that there are mission purposes which a children's club sets out to fulfil. Both the congregation and the club leaders need to support these mission objectives. The leader who is convinced by the purposes of the mission objectives and builds and trains a team of assistants and helpers to pursue those objectives will be fulfilling a ministry of Christian nurture and faith development of long term value in children's lives.

Will the local church have a children's club? If any congregation wishes to take seriously its ministry to and for children, it has an option to decide for club work. If it does so, let it be mindful of the missional purposes of club ministry and recruit and equip leaders who can embrace and deliver a club program that will fulfil those mission objectives.

The five points of the K.U.C.A. charter represent the succinct Christian objectives of club ministry to children. Such objectives cannot be met without intentionality from the congregation and personal conviction and preparation from the children's club leaders.

In the three chapters of Part 1, we have outlined principles from three perspectives: Jesus and the nurturing community; children as developing learners; and the club in the context of children's ministry. We draw these together in summary form.

PRINCIPLES FOR CHILDREN'S CLUB MINISTRY — A SUMMARY

Club leaders, congregations and church educators can confidently approach ministry to children through children's club work if these principles are acknowledged.

There are **theological principles** which undergird the work. We are called to minister to children because Jesus by word and deed clearly showed his care for and delight in children. He called them to him. He placed the child in the midst. The invitation is for children to belong to him, and with all Christians to grow toward Christian maturity and Christlikeness. The community of faith has a mutual ministry to nurture young and old in order to attain fullness in the measure of the stature of Christ. Work amongst children is to be valued as a ministry in Christ's name as children are called to our Lord as his disciples.

There are **developmental principles** to guide us in our ministry to children. Children of club age are not conceptual thinkers, but think in concrete terms. They have faith and are developing faith. There are age appropriate ways in which their mental, moral and spiritual development can be stimulated. Such ways will make much use of experiences, participation and involvement. Adults who show Christian living in real-life terms and who can engage children in imaginative and practical expression will foster their development. Club age children will grow with the help of sensitive leaders, aware of their developmental needs.

There are **church program principles** to guide us. To decide on the establishment of a church children's club is a deliberate decision. It is one means open to a congregation to exercise its ministry to children. The club has mission objectives that will require congregational support and ongoing commitment and leader conviction. Leaders have the responsibility to develop programs which will fulfil the mission objectives of a church children's club. The central objective of the club is to encourage children to trust Jesus Christ as their Saviour and Friend and to nurture them in their growing relationship with him.

These are the principles that provide the foundation upon which the practical leadership work will be established.

Notes

1. John Bodycomb, *A Matter of Death and Life: The Future of Australia's Churches*, Joint Board of Christian Education, Melbourne, 1986, p. 60.
2. David Merritt in Report of the Joint Board of Christian Education in David Gill, *Minutes of the Fifth Assembly*, May 22–28 1988, Uniting Church Press, Melbourne, 1988, p. 194.
3. Lawrence O. Richards, *A New Face for the Church*, Zondervan Publishing, Grand Rapids, 1970, pp. 248ff.
4. Official Member Charter Certificate, Kids of the Uniting Church in Australia, U.C.A. Synod Office, South Australia.

Chapter 5

Administration of a children's club

A club may have many good features but fall apart because it has not been administered well. Its affairs need to be directed and organised simply, unobtrusively and efficiently. Here are some observations.

1. The secret is to work out the level, or the amount, of administration required. A club needs just the right amount. Too much and there is unnecessary red-tape; too little and important matters are not attended to, or not considered.

2. Administrative procedures can be made to work for the club, to help it achieve its aims. For example, retaining current members and reaching out for new will be assisted by sound procedures in using a Club Register and Club Attendance Roll.

3. Holding and increasing membership may well depend on the shape of the club organisation. Will it, for example, be built around a central core of leader and assistants sharing the tasks, or will it use a leader with program conveners? Will it use permanent small groups with a leader attached to each? Or will it treat the club like a family group, and only use small groups for some activities, on some occasions?

4. There are highly important procedures which relate to the duty of care for other people's children, and to parental consent for membership and involvement. Because of the legal implications, a leader can not treat such administrative procedures lightly.

There are different aspects of administering and organising the affairs of a children's club. In this program we will concentrate on topics relating to organisational options for a club, records of membership and attendance, parental consents and information, supervision and security, financial arrangements, suitable venues, reporting, publicity and promotion, meals and suppers. There are several tasks to undertake, and a self-assessment activity, with your mentor, indicates the standards to which you can aim. In Chapter 7 'Pastoral care and faith development in a children's club', further attention is given to club organisation and small groups as they can help children in their growth. Other aspects of organisation are expanded in Chapter 9 'Leadership and team-building in a children's club'.

1 ORGANISATIONAL STRUCTURE OF A CHILDREN'S CLUB

No two clubs will have the same structure. Two models are suggested here, not because they are the only two ways, but because they represent two styles that would be appropriate in certain settings. One is simpler in appearance, but both require consistent involvement from the leaders to be effective.

How many adult leaders does a club need? A rule of thumb is to establish a leader team of sufficient size to give you a ratio of one leader to every six children, at least. So for a membership of twenty-four children you need at least four leaders. If you are using older teenagers as some of your leaders, then the ratio should be 1:6, plus one or two extra.

The first style can be called the *leader and assistants* model. The method calls for the leader to enlist two adult assistants, with two or three older teenagers as junior assistants. Figure 1 depicts the style in chart form.

The leader, the adult assistants and the junior assistants, form the team who conduct the club. They share leadership between them; for example, one may lead a game, one will tell the story, two plan and conduct the craft, and another leads the worship. Next meeting each may tackle a different task. They help each other to gain experience. They train each other. They plan the meetings and the program content together. They support each other while one of them is leading the children. When groups are formed, either on a temporary or permanent basis, then each works with a group.

The members of a team of this type will depend on each other a great deal. Such a team could successfully conduct a club with perhaps up to thirty-six members.

The second style can be called the *leader and executive conveners* model. In this type of

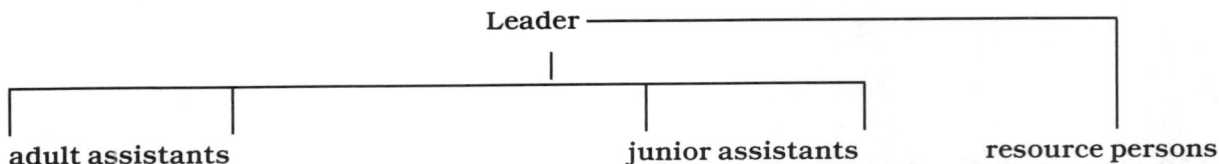

Fig. 1

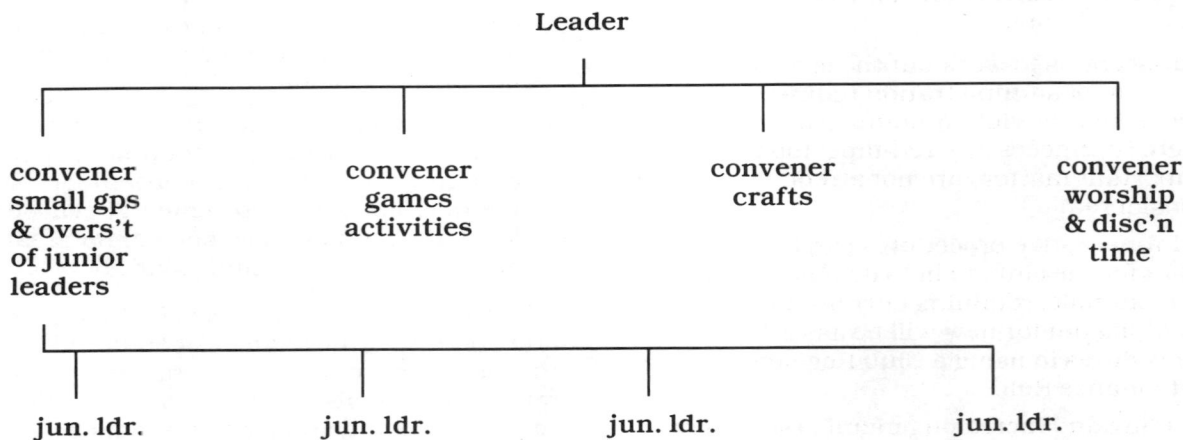

Fig. 2

organisation, the leader heads a team of adults who are selected as conveners for specific tasks in the club. Figure 2 indicates the specialities which the conveners adopt.

Each person will have specific responsibilites. The conveners are specialists, the leader and the conveners form the executive, and they do the broad planning. The conveners contribute plans and strategies from their areas of interest. The planning meetings dovetail the plans. The leader has to 'steer the ship', especially to ensure that the faith development aims of the club are being actively pursued.

This model allows for permanent small groups to which children are allotted, and which have a junior leader as their guide. One convener has oversight of these groups, and the training of the junior leaders. Each of the conveners would lean heavily on the junior leaders for assistance in their various activities.

This is a model that requires job delegation, but it is well suited to large clubs that have a pool of willing and experienced adults, and that set out to train junior leaders in club work.

Which model is yours? It may be more similar to one than the other. Or is yours a 'one person does everything' type? If so, your immediate priority will be to recruit other assistants and helpers, for the sake of the children and for the sake of the church's work.

Task

Can you describe the shape of the organisation of your club? In what ways could your present arrangements be improved? Draw a simple diagram of your club's organisational plan, and discuss its advantages and disadvantages with your mentor.

2 CLUB MEMBERSHIP REGISTER

There has to be some paper work in a club. The important matter is to make it work for you. There is one set of records that will be invaluable to you in meeting parents, coming to know the children, and in offering programs of interest. The club needs to have a Membership Register.

Use a loose leaf, ring folder. Draw up pages similar to the Register Sheet depicted on page 44, and photocopy the quantity you need. As each child joins and you meet the parents, you will be able to record details of your new members. You need to know correct names, addresses and telephone numbers. The register will give you the vital information on birthdays. It is an advantage to know where each child goes to school, and what the child's interests, sports and hobbies are.

The register will help you know who your children are. Oversight, outreach, and retention of members will be enhanced if you use your register in a methodical way, regularly thumbing through it, and individually remembering each child.

Task

Does your club have a register? Make one if you have not done this already. You can design your own sheets, or photocopy the sample provided. When you have it completed, up to date, with a page for each child in the club, show it to you mentor.

3 ATTENDANCE ROLL

The purpose of an Attendance Roll is to help you notice the children who are present, and also those who are absent. The roll is not designed to make extra work for you, but rather to establish patterns of attendance.

Retaining members is important. Finding new members is important. If a child is missing, it always helps if the leader knows. Is it because of sickness, or holidays, or loss of interest? If it is a loss of interest, it may be a program problem, or it may be because the child is having difficulty with another child at the club, or there may be factors at school or home. On some occasions, it may be because of the inability of parents to bring the child because of work hours.

An Attendance Roll can be drawn up using an exercise book, or you may prefer to buy a ready made product. All that is needed is a grid, with children's names down one side, and the meeting dates across the top.

What do you do if children miss meetings? Sometimes you will know the reasons because an apology has been sent, or other children from the family tell you, or playmates from school tell you of children's sickness. If an absence is unexplained over several meetings then follow-up will be necessary.

These are the patterns of care:

- that the Roll is marked regularly
- that you review the Roll after each meeting
- that you, or another member of the team, follow-up children.

Task

Do you have a club Attendance Roll book? Commence one, and keep on using it. You can delegate a team member to mark it, but retrieve it at the end of each meeting, so you can have your finger on the attendance. Arrange for follow-up visits as needed. Show your roll book to your mentor.

4 PARENTAL INFORMATION AND AGREEMENT PROCEDURES

There are several important administrative procedures that relate to parents or guardians. Procedures which relate to 'consent' are of the highest importance. Broadly these are the areas:

1. Procedures that seek parents' interest and possible involvement or assistance to the club;

2. Procedures to ensure that parents are agreeable for their child to belong to the club, and are supportive of its aims and principles;

3. Procedures that ensure parents give permission for the leader to act in any medical emergency, and indemnify the leaders concerning any actions they need to take when the child is in their care.

Let us examine these areas in turn. We begin by emphasising the *parent's right to information about the club* and its activities.

The leader needs to remember constantly that parents need to know about the club and its activities, and especially so if you wish a meeting or meetings to happen elsewhere. Parents need to be given information, but also need to have ways to ask questions.

It is a sensible administrative procedure to give parents an information sheet or leaflet about the club at the time when they give permission for their child to join. Even a one-page information sheet will be valuable. The sheet should include:

- the accurate name of the club
- the age group for which the club caters

- the aims of the club. These could be the aims as described on the KUCA charter. By this means parents are quite clear that this is a church club, and that it has missional purposes.
- the details of insurance cover in regard to public liability, and to personal accident cover; if there is none, parents need to know that medical benefits or school insurances may have to be used.
- the need for parents to give signed permission for the child to belong
- the notice that for outings, camps, etc., special information and consent forms will be provided, with the understanding that no child will be permitted to go on such an activity unless a parental consent form is completed and held by the leader. For camps, especially, information about the child's health will also be required, with specific instructions in writing concerning any medication being used by a child.
- the expectation that the child will attend regularly
- clear details about names and telephone numbers of at least two of the adult leaders, and the telephone number of the parish office, or of the minister.

These items can be framed in friendly language, and should not be made to sound legalistic or threatening. But such an information sheet will show that your club is properly conducted, and that the leaders are well aware of their responsibilities.

For an outing, activity or camp, it is important to give parents information, as well as have a form that gives parental consent for the child to attend. These specific details will be required:

- accurate information about assembly times and places, and the time of arrival or return. Indicate whether children are to be picked up from a specific place, or whether the leaders will have children taken home
- details about the types of activities
- accurate details about where the activity is to take place. If it is an overnight activity, such as a camp, details of the address and contact telephone numbers are essential
- explain clearly what children are to bring, especially in regard to food, clothes or money
- information is needed about transport — bus, train, private car, etc. If it is by private car, then both the law and parents will expect seat-belt enforcement, and no more persons in a car than is legally permitted. There must also be car insurance.

We consider now the important procedure of gaining *parental consent*. Because leaders are standing in for parents, the leaders have a duty of care for the children to act responsibly. If an emergency arises, however, you must be able to act. Your authority to take action is a signed consent form from a parent or guardian. In certain emergencies, medical authorities may ask to see such written consent.

This may seem rather legalistic but all organisations working with children have to comply with such arrangements. Insurance companies, in particular, will expect sound administrative procedures in this regard if there are claims to be dealt with.

Consent forms should contain statements such as these.

SAMPLE

Parent's agreement and authority

I/We consent to our son/daughter ....

.... becoming a member of the

.... Club.

I/We will encourage him/her to attend regularly, to pay the subscriptions promptly, and to abide by the rules of the club.

If during any activity, urgent medical attention is required by my/our child, I/We authorise the leader in charge to take such action as may be necessary and I/We agree to indemnify the

.... Church and its authorised officials from all responsibility thereto.

Signed ....

.... Date: ....
Parent/Guardian

For a special event, where the club meets elsewhere, or goes on a ramble, or visits a place of interest, or is to spend a week-end in camp, a special *parent's consent* form should be prepared, signed by each parent or guardian, and carrried with you on the event. As well, parents should have been given specific information about the event. A child should not be taken if there is no consent form signed. It is also most important to note that a junior leader who is not yet eighteen is a minor under law, and therefore should also furnish a signed parental consent form.

Remember that these are not legalisms required by the church, but have arisen through society's demands for accountability. It is foolish to think 'nothing will happen to us' or 'the parents of my children are not ones to worry'. A serious accident, or a mishap through negligence, or a child's impetuous or reckless actions could make all the difference. As a leader you will want to take a responsible attitude to the oversight of other people's children. Part of that responsibility is to have the necessary protection and freedom to act.

We turn now to a procedure aimed to foster *parent's involvement* in the club. Some parents will have an interest in helping in some way. They may not be forward in offering, however. There are times when you will need to find transport, or have extra helpers on a meeting night, or extra supervision on a day outing. You could also find amongst parents those whose occupations, interests, sports or hobbies could provide interesting segments in programs.

One way of finding out these things is to ask them at the time when they enrol their child. You can give them a form at the same time as you hand over the club information sheet, as you complete the club register sheet, and as they sign the parent's consent form. A sample form can be found on page 44. By this means they can tell you what their interests are, and what their capacities and willingness may be to offer specific support. You would keep these sheets on permanent file, and refer to them regularly. If people show keenness to be involved, make sure you use them at the earliest possible time, and continue to cultivate the interest of all the parents.

Task

Here are two items. Choose one of them. Either prepare your own version of a *parent's consent* form, along the lines of the sample, and begin using it. Or, prepare a *parent's consent* form for a special occasion when the club will be on an outing, or meeting elsewhere. Make sure that it gives details of the event, allows parents to give permission for their child to attend, and gives the leader in charge authority to act in an emergency. Show your finished product to your mentor, and check through the details.

5 FINANCIAL MATTERS

Different clubs will have different financial arrangements, according to the types of support arranged by the congregation. But all clubs have to deal with money, and need to do so with due responsibility.

Therefore the club leader will appoint, or see that a treasurer is appointed, to handle the financial affairs of the club. The club will also need a bank account, with withdrawals requiring two out of three signatures. The treasurer will maintain a simple set of books, which will be audited annually, and which should comply with the standards set by the denomination. Receipts will be written for all cash income and donations, and money is banked. A petty cash float is held for the week-by-week essentials.

The leaders, no doubt, will decide if it will finance its operation by donations from children, and from the councils of the congregation or parish, or if it will establish a regular subscription as a sign of membership, with set amounts paid at each meeting.

The only fair way to set a subscription is for the leader and the treasurer to work out a budget. A budget will set down on paper answers to two questions.

a) What items of expense can we expect this club to face over the next twelve months? The list will include craft materials, books, games equipment, rent, electricity contributions, gifts to parish, presbytery, synod, supper expenses, etc. The amount per item is estimated.

b) What levels of income can we expect to receive over the next twelve months? This will include donations, interest, money raising activities. Subscriptions are estimated and placed on the income side.

Being mindful of the anticipated expenses, then the size of the required income becomes clear. By noting the number of members, then a calculation can be made to set a subscription fee, which, though perhaps not covering all expenses, will allow all to take a fair share.

The club leader and the treasurer will recognise that parents are willing to pay a subscription for their child's membership. It should be a realistic figure (depending on the nature of the community) but should not be exorbitant.

Because the club is handling money in the name of the church, and largely contributed by younger families, it is wise to be careful with financial arrangements. The brown paper bag of loose cash is not careful enough!

Although the club needs an appointed treasurer, does it also need a secretary? Generally, a secretary in the formal sense may not be required. The program book is the best record of the discussions at plannings meetings. But there are letters to write, and notices to prepare, and for this work a member of the team may volunteer, or a resource person from the parents or congregation may be willing to assist the leader team with these matters. If you have a staffed parish church office, then help from that source may be possible.

Task

Discuss with your mentor how the financial arrangements of your club have been established. Are there improvements you believe should be made? What are your plans?

---

6 SUPERVISION OF CHILDREN

Children's club leaders often wish they had eyes in the back of their heads, because of the need to provide leadership, get ready for the program and supervise children all at the same time.

For this reason it is sensible to share out supervision amongst the team. As they arrive, children need to be greeted and introduced to some activity. Some clubs have established small groups with a leader attached to each, and these will have an activity to occupy them before the meeting begins. Others have a supervised game, such as 'continuous cricket' in which any member and any number can participate, as they arrive. On other occasions, there may be displays for children to look at. The idea is to avoid, if you can, children being left to their own devices. Neither do you want children to be asked to sit down to wait. Supervision can be low key, but it is easier and safer to supervise children involved in an activity, than it is to keep an eye on them running wild.

During the program, there will be plenty to do, and everyone shares in the supervision. At the close of the meeting, care is again needed to ensure that supervision is adequate. Of course, these children are old enough not to run out onto the road, or are they? Supervision of continuing play can be unobtrusive, but it needs to be there. The leaders need to ensure that children have gone home with the right adult, and not with a neighbour, and not with a stranger.

For these reasons, the leaders, through the leaders' planning meetings, need to have planned for supervision of children, from the time the first one arrives until the last one has left with a parent or guardian. It is a good plan to have one leader who is the post-meeting supervisor, whilst another is there to talk with parents, even briefly, before they take their children and leave.

First aid and first aider

There should be a first aid kit available at the meeting place. The grazed knuckle or knee may be the most serious injuries to be dealt with, but the kit is needed. Smaller kits which could also be taken on outings, would be quite suitable. Ready made kits are available, or you can make up your own. Your kit should contain these items at least: small scissors, splinter forceps, needle, safety pins, small bowl, cotton wool, band-aid strips, gauze bandages (several widths), triangular bandage, sanitary napkins, strapping (adhesive strip dressing), antiseptic, antiseptic cream, burn cream, and soluble asprin. If going to camp, there would be other items of a medicine chest type, which may be useful.

It is also an advantage to have one of the leader team designated as first aider. A person who has trained with the St John Ambulance Brigade or the Red Cross, and who holds a basic first aid qualification, would be excellent in this role. Why? Because the designated first aider will act without being asked, will know what to do, will know their limitations, will know when more than first aid is required, and will do it without fuss. It is a piece of precautionary planning in a well administered club.

7 THE MEETING PLACE

It is usually presumed that when a children's club is to be formed, that it will meet in the church hall. You will want to check out the facility, however, because some church halls are not suited to children's club work. Some are so large that it is hard to feel comfortable with their echoes and spaciousness. Some have highly polished floors that are difficult or dangerous to run about on. Some have floors so old that splinters are easily 'caught'. Some have heavy pews for seating which are impossible for children to move.

So check out the meeting place. If it is not suitable, give your reasons and diplomatically suggest improvements. Ideally the meeting place should include these features:

- there are male and female toilets, indoors and well lit
- there are kitchen facilities with crockery and utensils sufficient for the club
- the floor is safe for playing games, and for sitting on. Preferably there is a carpet square for story and worship times
- there are work tables that are stable, and in sufficient quantity for all children to have a work space
- there are chairs, light enough for children to move, and which can be set against the walls quickly
- the space is uncluttered by other gear
- the playing and meeting space is large enough for games, but small enough for a family feeling
- there is a secure storage cupboard for the club to lock away playing equipment and craft materials, for the sake of tidiness as much as security and the avoidance of mis-use.

The meeting place will not reach the ideal in many places, but forethought and co-operation may improve the facility for club use. In negotiating the needs of the club for a suitable venue, it will be wise to ascertain whether the club is expected to contribute towards running costs. If so, these estimates need to be included in the budget calculations. Should the club pay? There are arguments either way. The church wants the club as part of its community, for the children, their parents, and for outreach, but so do the parents, who will be willing to subscribe for their children's activities. If there is some payment or donation, it perhaps helps to spread the load. The policies of the church towards its other activities, fellowships and groups will have a bearing on what is worked out locally.

8 REPORTING — COMMUNICATING

It will be a regular part of the leader's responsibility to report to the Council of Elders, or to the minister, about the progress of the club. The reporting may be done through a designated elder, verbally or in writing, or in person at the council. This could be seen as a burden, or it can be seen as a good opportunity for children's work to be given value and attention.

Your report should inform about these factors:

- the membership patterns — regular, falling, rising attendance, new members
- the leader team strength — is it adequate in size, is further recruitment required?
- the need for resource support — people, materials, finances
- your perception of the atmosphere and program of the club, and its effectiveness in fostering the faith development of the children
- your recommendations for increasing the linkages between the congregation and the children's club within the community of faith for the ultimate strengthening of the work of the kingdom.

Enthusiasm begets enthusiasm. Speak enthusiastically. Especially with the congregation at worship, take the opportunities boldly to identify the club, to have the children participate in Sunday worship as a club, to display photographs of club activities, and to give the congregation pride in the growth of their children. That will help greatly in enthusing further leadership and membership drives.

If you can enlist the elders to help you promote the club to the wider community, then promotion will raise the profile of the club further. Letterbox drops in the locality, bright posters on shopping centre notice boards, in schools, community health centres, welfare offices and local government council facilities may all help the community know that your club cares about children. Show that your club can offer a sound, disciplined, enjoyable involvement for children in a Christian atmosphere.

Task

Mock-up a design for an A4 sized poster that would be suitable for a public centre, and would give parents the essential information about your children's club. Will it include sketches, information sources, telephone numbers, meeting place address and times, subscription costs, and what else? For now, discuss with your mentor how you could use such posters in your locality. Explain how you would try to enlist the elders and the congregation in this project. Keep a note of the ideas and plans, and put it into action when the time is right.

9 MEALS AND SUPPERS

Some clubs have a meal as part of their meeting time. This allows the meeting to begin earlier, but it also requires the organisation of a meal. There are some advantages and some disadvantages in having a regular meal.

Advantages

- the meeting can begin earlier, and finish at a better time for younger children
- it gives time for leaders to sit and talk with children
- it is a way for utilising the support of resource people who may not be suited to club leadership
- parents can be confident that the children will have an adequate meal.

Disadvantages

- the commitment to meal preparation, table layout, clearing and cleaning for every meeting is considerable
- the earlier start is inconvenient for people not yet home from work, and this includes club leaders
- the overall program needs to be carefully timed to obviate slack times — when children may have nothing to do between the meal and commencement of the activity program. Some free time is useful and beneficial; too much and accidents occur.
- it is not easy to find a menu which pleases all, or indeed most, children.

It is a local decision, however. If a meal is included, then good organisation is required. Here are some pointers:

- appoint a meal co-ordinator who is not on the program team
- use resource helpers to form a catering team. These are not used in other parts of the organisation
- choose a menu in which food is nutritious, and simple to prepare. Use the catering resource team to research a menu by consulting parents
- conduct the meal with control. Use rules about seeking permission to leave the table. Insist on table manners.
- use shared graces, so that children learn the words of gratitude
- serve helpings which are child sized
- ensure that costs are covered, by subscriptions or specific meal payments.

Suppers

It is not necessary, even in a club which does

not use a meal, to have supper at every meeting. Bed-going habits of children vary. Some parents would prefer their children not to have drinks close to bed time. Others do not mind. Generally, however, these are decisions best made by the parents at home.

But for special events in the club, an extra dimension will be added if supper is part of the program. It should be kept simple, however. A cup of hot chocolate, or a glass of fruit juice, or cordial, and a small rock bun or similar, may be quite sufficient. Avoid coffee and tea. For a 'dress-up' program, the drinks and eats can be somewhat special. Give the items new names, new colourings, and a little special flair to relate to the theme.

10 USEFUL RESOURCES

The subjects of child safety, small organisation management and finance and other such matters are of concern to other organisations too. Thus you may find useful resources by enquiring from other youth organisations.

Government departments handling recreation, sport or youth affairs or Councils of Social Service (non-government) often produce booklets on club finances, insurance, planning and administration.

These resources can be a useful addition to this learning program. Note also people in the congregation who may have experience or contacts that could assist you in any aspects of club administration.

11 THE CLUB LEADER ADMINISTERS THE CHILDREN'S CLUB

This program has given attention to the administrative matters for which the club leader is responsible. Although the procedures and organisational approaches of a well administered club are not often acknowledged, the absence of such careful procedures become noticeable quickly.

If administration is poorly conducted or forgotten, there is the possibility of serious difficulty. This is especially so in the areas of parental information and consent. Leaders need to know without doubt that they have parents' consent for their children's involvement in the club and its special activities. Nods of the head are not enough. Given the present legal and insurance climate, signed consent forms are required.

A well run club will have these items attended to, and the procedures will be kept alive constantly. They will be part and parcel of the leader's work. That is the type of leader who gains the trust of the parents and the church.

The following check list will be a reminder to you of these necessary administrative tasks and standards. A well run club will have local procedures developed to meet these standards.

SELF-ASSESSMENT

When you have completed the tasks outlined in this learning program, you will be ready for this assessment activity with the aid of your mentor.

It is a joint activity, with conversation, through which your mentor will endorse the completion of tasks. The mentor will be looking at your activities in the club, and helping you assess whether you performed the various functions according to the suggested standards.

Levels of performance: Place an 'X' in the appropriate box. If, because of special circumstances, a component was not applicable, or impossible to execute, an 'X' may be placed in the 'not applicable' box. All items should receive either a N/A, good or excellent response. If any item receives a 'none, poor or fair' response, then you and the mentor will need to determine what additional activities are required to complete the component. It may mean revising a procedure, and then inviting your mentor to observe aspects of your administration again. The aim is a personal one — to administer the affairs of a children's club efficiently, with the care and safety of children uppermost.

Rating scale (each item): N/A | None | Poor | Fair | Good | Excellent

1. As leader, I describe the organisational model on which the club is built, in terms of:
   a. how leaders and helpers are used ☐☐☐☐☐☐
   b. how essential jobs are shared ☐☐☐☐☐☐
   c. how the organisation fits the size of the club ☐☐☐☐☐☐

2. As leader, I have achieved a ratio of one leader to each six children, or better. ☐☐☐☐☐☐

3. As leader, I maintain, accurately, a club membership register. ☐☐☐☐☐☐

4. As leader, I maintain, accurately, following each meeting, a club attendance roll. ☐☐☐☐☐☐

5. As leader, I hold for each child a parental agreement form which includes
   a. parent's consent for the child to attend ☐☐☐☐☐☐
   b. parent's consent for the leader to seek urgent medical attention ☐☐☐☐☐☐
   c. agreement that the child will follow the directions of leader/s and abide by the rules of the club ☐☐☐☐☐☐
   d. a clause by which parent/s/guardians indemnify leaders. ☐☐☐☐☐☐

6. As leader, I ensure that on every occasion when the club meets away from the regular venue, that
   a. a signed parental consent form is held for each child and junior leader ☐☐☐☐☐☐
   b. the consent form includes . . .
      parental consent ☐☐☐☐☐☐
      permission is given to seek urgent medical attention. ☐☐☐☐☐☐

7. As leader, I provide parents enrolling children with a club information sheet which . . .
   a. gives information about the club ☐☐☐☐☐☐
   b. seeks parent's willingness to assist the club. ☐☐☐☐☐☐

8. As leader, I ensure that . . .
   a. a club treasurer is appointed ☐☐☐☐☐☐
   b. the club has a bank account ☐☐☐☐☐☐
   c. withdrawals require two of three signatures ☐☐☐☐☐☐
   d. that receipts are written for all cash income. ☐☐☐☐☐☐

9. As leader, I with the treasurer, annually
   a. draw up a club budget ☐☐☐☐☐☐
   b. set the members' subscription fee. ☐☐☐☐☐☐

10. As leader, I ensure that the treasurer
    a. maintains a current record of income and expenditure ☐☐☐☐☐☐
    b. submits an annual, audited record of income and expenditure. ☐☐☐☐☐☐

11. As leader, I provide at each meeting
    a. supervision as children arrive ☐☐☐☐☐☐

	N/A	None	Poor	Fair	Good	Excellent
b. supervision of children throughout program and free time	☐	☐	☐	☐	☐	☐
c. supervision of children leaving meeting ensuring each child is in care of appropriate person	☐	☐	☐	☐	☐	☐
d. supervision continues until the last child has left safely.	☐	☐	☐	☐	☐	☐
12 As leader, I ensure that at each meeting, outing or event, there is						
a. a designated first-aider	☐	☐	☐	☐	☐	☐
b. a first-aid kit.	☐	☐	☐	☐	☐	☐
13 As leader, I ensure that the club meeting place has						
a. suitable male and female toilets, well lit, preferably accessible from inside the building	☐	☐	☐	☐	☐	☐
b. kitchen facilities	☐	☐	☐	☐	☐	☐
c. safe playing floor	☐	☐	☐	☐	☐	☐
d. sufficient, suitable work tables	☐	☐	☐	☐	☐	☐
e. chairs which are easily moved	☐	☐	☐	☐	☐	☐
f. secure storage cupboard.	☐	☐	☐	☐	☐	☐
14 As leader, I report on the state of the club to the Council of Elders, regularly, as required locally.	☐	☐	☐	☐	☐	☐
15 As leader, I liaise with Presbytery and Synod Children's Ministry bodies in order to . . .						
a. report directory details	☐	☐	☐	☐	☐	☐
b. seek training information	☐	☐	☐	☐	☐	☐

	N/A	Fair	Poor	None	Good	Excellent
c. pursue resources.	☐	☐	☐	☐	☐	☐
16 As leader, I promote the club, verbally, in writing, and in publicity form to . . .						
a. the congregation	☐	☐	☐	☐	☐	☐
b. schools in the community	☐	☐	☐	☐	☐	☐
c. community agencies.	☐	☐	☐	☐	☐	☐
17 As leader, I ensure that, if a meal is a regular part of the club program,						
a. a meal co-ordinator is appointed	☐	☐	☐	☐	☐	☐
b. a catering team is formed	☐	☐	☐	☐	☐	☐
c. food is nutritious	☐	☐	☐	☐	☐	☐
d. serves are child-sized	☐	☐	☐	☐	☐	☐
e. costs are covered	☐	☐	☐	☐	☐	☐
f. Grace is shared	☐	☐	☐	☐	☐	☐
g. table manners are insisted on.	☐	☐	☐	☐	☐	☐
18 As leader, I ensure that when a supper is served, at an evening meeting						
a. drinks are appropriate for children	☐	☐	☐	☐	☐	☐
b. food is simple and light.	☐	☐	☐	☐	☐	☐

Mentor's endorsement

I declare that (leader's name) .... has completed the self-assessment task of this learning program with good or excellent markings.

Signed .... (Mentor) .... **(Date)**

Club register sheet

Child

Surname: ....

Given names: ....

Preferred name: ....

Address: ....

....

Post Code: .... Telephone No. ....

School attended: ....

Religion: ....

Date of birth: .... Date of joining: ....

Interests, pastimes, hobbies, sports: ....

....

Physical needs, special care: ....

....

Parents

Father's initials:	Mother's initials:
....	....
Occupation:	Occupation: ....
....	....
Interests, hobbies, sports:	Interests, hobbies, sports:
....	....

Notes:

Parent survey

Family name: ....

Given names: ....
Mother/Guardian

....
Father/Guardian

The leaders of the .... children's club would welcome your involvement as parent/s, from time to time, in the life of the club. We are sure that your child would also enjoy this.
How could you help? Would you be willing, on occasions to: (please tick as applicable)

- assist with transport
- assist with supervision
- assist as a leader, helper or instructor
- assist with money raising
- assist with outings, or trips, or camps
- assist with occasional suppers
- assist children to learn about your own hobbies, work, skills, sports or interests.

Here is a list of interests and hobbies. Would you indicate any in which you would be able to share knowledge with children.

Aboriginal lore	Folk songs	Outback life
Australian birds	Gardening	Painting
	Geology	Pottery
Astronomy	Games	Plays/skits
Beadwork	Handcrafts	Puppetry
Bible	Health	Puzzles
Candlemaking	Jewelry making	Papier mâché
Clay-work		Photography
Codes	Kite flying	Pets
Collections	Languages	Quizzes
Cooking	Macrame	Radio
Emergency services	Maskmaking	Recording
	Mapping	Singing
Cycling	Machines	Sports
Camping	Mapping	Swimming
Conservation	Model boats	Tie-dying
Dance	Model planes	Travels
Drama	Model cars	Weather
Electricity	Nature observation	Whipping-tops
Ethnic lore		
Farm life	Music making	Woodwork
Fishing	Nutcraft	Any others:
First aid	Lapidary	
Fire services	Ornaments	

When you have completed both sides, and signed the parent's consent please return this sheet to club leader .... with thanks.
(*Note*: the parent's consent form is on page 37.)

Chapter 6

Conducting children's club programs

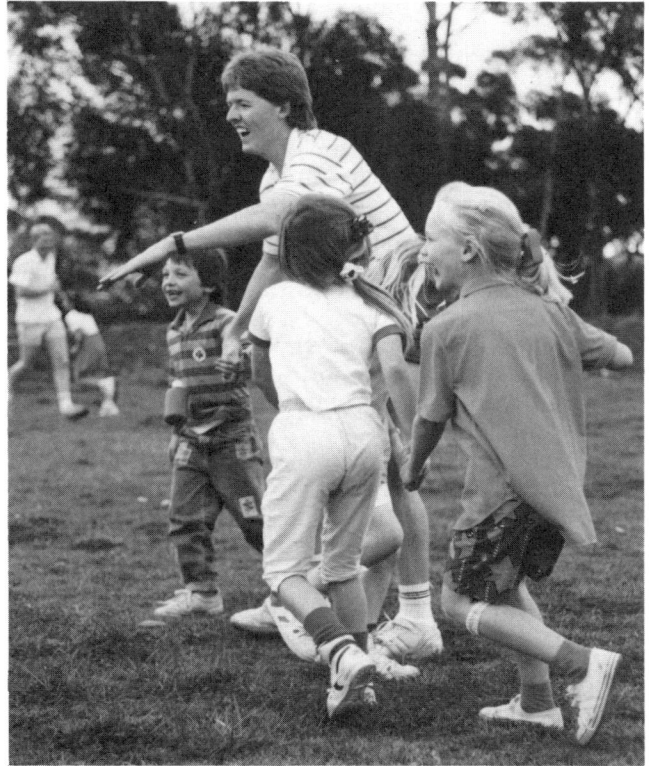

'What shall we do tonight?' If the club leader wakes up in the morning with that question in mind, two things are likely to happen. First, a hastily-thrown-together program will result, which will be stale because it will use material on top of the leader's memory. And second, that may begin a series of ill-prepared and unplanned programs, causing children to lose interest and to leave. Vibrant programs can fill a club; lack of such programs will empty it.

The secret of successful children's clubs is programs with vitality, interest and content that raise enthusiasm. Such programs claim the interest of children, but they only happen with planning, attention to content, and detailed preparation. Other factors are important, of course, such as leadership, friendship and individual recognition. Other learning programs in this series will attend to those issues. Let us now concentrate on 'program planning' and 'conducting programs'.

In this learning program, we want to:
- describe methods for long and short term program planning
- describe essential qualities or ingredients in a church children's club program
- list guidelines for the effective conduct of the various elements of programs.

1 HOW TO PLAN PROGRAMS

The first step is to use a *Program Book* which is simply a ringed folder with loose pages and several sections. The *Program Book* will be your aid to planning long and short term.

How do we proceed? The book will be divided into three unequal parts.

Part 1 will have an Annual Planner with a year long calendar, and a calendar for next year as well.

Part 2 will have a page for each term of the year.

Part 3 will have a specifically prepared set of pages, one for each meeting. This section will be the largest.

How to use these parts? In Part 1, you will note all the meeting dates for the year on the planner. You will note when church festivals are, or public holidays, or celebrations, or school term dates. You will note when Sunday school events will fall, when a family camp is proposed, or when kids' camp-out will be held. Part 1 is designed to give you an overview of the year. As soon as fixtures are announced, you note the details. You can avoid clashes, and you prepare in time for events.

In Part 2, you and your team progressively write in the aims or ideas you have on one of the term sheets. Ideas are suggested which you do not want to forget, but which do not need to be worked on for three or four months; such ideas are writen in a sheet in Part 2. On each term sheet you will also transfer information from the Part 1 planner. The term sheets become a series of notes about events to attend, or events to steer around, or aims for the club to achieve, or ideas for a theme to develop in an evening program. If you have heard of someone in the congregation or the community who would be of interest to the club members, then you record the details. You may not be able to use all the material you have noted in Part 2 of your *Program Book*, but the notations become a seedbed for the germination of ideas.

In Part 3 of the *Program Book*, you will use specially drawn sheets, one for each meeting. Draw up the sheets to your own requirements, and photocopy the quantity you need. A sample is provided on page 62. Each sheet will be dated (from Part 1), and each sheet will have relevant notes transferred from Part 2 term sheets. Thus notes about what to prepare for, what to include in the content, and what to announce in notices can be recorded. Also notes about children's birthdays (information will come from your club register) can be written in, in advance.

Particularly, Part 3 sheets will contain the details of the program for the occasion. You can work ahead, writing in the names of games, stories, craft ideas, and so on, as you discover them and can see an appropriate time for using them. Each sheet will show:

- the items that make up the program, in program order
- the name of the leader who is responsible for conducting each segment

- the equipment that each segment requires
- the time allowed for each segment.

You will take a flexible approach to running each program, of course. But because you have come to the meeting with a planned program, which the other leaders are also aware of and can refer to, then there is no reason for leaders to wonder about what happens next. It has been planned in some detail. This approach will avoid children being left to run, because leaders are still deciding! Effective programs, well planned beforehand, are the major eliminators of mischief.

Long and short term program planning results in detailed program content. The secrets are:

- look ahead, a long way
- commit the ideas or information to paper in your *Program Book*
- look closely, at each individual program
- write the details down in a business like manner
- use your *Program Book* as a tool. Let it help you take a methodical approach to program planning, and help you to prepare programs in detail
- 'plan your work, and work your plan' says the old adage. The wisdom is relevant for program planning also.

Task

Prepare a *Program Book* with its three sections. Begin to use it immediately. Show your mentor.

Our next concern, of course, is to consider what content meeting programs should have.

2 HOW TO DECIDE WHAT GOES IN A PROGRAM FOR A MEETING

Effective children's club programs, with primary age children, meet certain criteria. There are many different types of content which will help the program meet these criteria. We certainly want to prevent our programs from becoming dull or lop-sided or single-tracked.

Here are twelve principles for effective programs.

1. Effective programs have a sense of purpose. They seek objectives. They want to go somewhere in particular.

2. Effective programs have continuity. In the long term, they proceed from one to another. In the individual program, there are linkages. The parts belong together.

3. Effective programs expand the child's world. They enhance children's lives. Children discover and learn.

4. Effective programs are fun meetings. It is enjoyable to belong and participate.

5. Effective programs have variety. The contents include some quiet, some busy, some craft, some quiet worship, some joyous singing, some conversation, some listening, some frantic and boisterous participation.

6. Effective programs are designed within themselves to lead to a high point, but then to taper down and quieten as the program concludes and children leave for home.

7. Effective programs provide a balance over time so that each element is given due weight, and so that many children's interests are given space.

8. Effective programs include contrasts. Children need noise and movement, so the program provides for them. Children also benefit from times of slowing down, to relax and listen.

9. Effective programs start and finish on time. Parents come to expect punctuality.

10. Effective programs use the time fully. There are no blank spaces where leaders and members wonder what to do. It is better to have more planned than can be achieved, than to have children at a loose end.

11. Effective programs provide human warmth. Leaders and children are friends. The leaders exercise control and set limits, but they are fair, firm and friendly.

12. Effective programs are a vehicle for witnessing to the love of Christ which pervades the life of the club in all its activities and relationships.

Leaders, in conducting programs, need to become keen observers of children's reactions and responses to program elements. Generally, leaders can learn much by watching, listening and conversing with children about how they think and react, and discovering what their interests are. There are two particular points to note.

1. *Noise*: children find noise satisfying and seem to thrive on it — up to a point. Children need legitimate outlets for noise-making. The program can allow noise, but not all the time. Leaders allow noise, but then direct and control it.

2. *Safety*: children in their exuberance and impetuosity may run themselves into trouble. Through lack of experience they may not appreciate unsafe actions. The leader anticipates this possibility, and ensures that the meeting place is safe, supervision is adequate, and that energy can be used within the program itself.

We can turn from principles upon which program planning is based, to consider the content of programs.

3 WHAT ARE THE INGREDIENTS OF A CHURCH CHILDREN'S CLUB PROGRAM?

Here is a list of ingredients. Not all are essential in every meeting, of course, but from their use well-balanced individual programs can come.

- games
- stories
- craft activity
- special events
- occasional meals, suppers
- prayers, devotions, worship
- learning or discovery times
- singing
- dress-up themes
- opening and closing ceremonies.

In this chapter, we will examine games, stories, crafts, discovery times, singing, dress-up themes, and opening and closing ceremonies. Prayers, devotions, Bible reading and worship will be given detailed treatment in Chapter 7 'Pastoral care and faith development in a children's club'.

Before considering these topics, it is wise to suggest ways and means for gaining children's attention in a club program. This represents a basic rule for the club.

4 CONTROLLING A MEETING

A leader cannot explain rules for a game, or tell a story, or introduce a newcomer, if the children are noisy, unruly, or not all in the same place. The leader needs to establish a method for bringing the club to order, ready to give attention. The method or methods need to be established as the rule of the club, and pride taken in the speed with which the rule is followed.

Here are four possible ways. In each case these are signs that each person must stand still, be quiet, and listen for the next instruction.

First method: the leader holds a hand above the head. Each child does the same until all have the message for stillness.

Second method: the leader calls out 'Kuca', almost like a 'coo-ee' call.

Third method: the leader uses hand claps to gain attention.

Fourth method: The leader uses a whistle. (This has the disadvantage of shrillness indoors, and makes the club meeting sound more like a football game.)

By using a sign, the children become still, ready for the next announcement. The leader should not attempt to begin talking until all the children have responded. Show that you expect quietness immediately after the sign is used. Then speak in a normal volume and tone. Shouting above noise is counter productive. Compliment the children who respond quickly. Make a game of it, and the club will become proud of its quick responses. 'We beat our own record. Well done!' Now to games.

5 GAMES IN PROGRAMS

Games will have a positive impact in the well-being of the club, provided you use some basic principles in choosing and conducting games. Inappropriate, poorly conducted or inadequately supervised games can make members and leaders dissatisfied. Here are some principles and guidelines that can help you as a leader to make good choices about games.

What is the value of games?

Children will learn through any well-run game. They will learn:

- skills using hands, eyes, memory, reasoning
- co-ordination of muscles, mind, movements
- attitudinal values of co-operation, team work, concepts of fair play and love in action
- specific knowledge if the games deal with facts to learn, such as Bible games
- self-discipline and personal development
- that participation is more important than competition, or winning or losing.

And the lesson of enjoyment together is a positive factor. All these are significant areas of learning in knowledge, skills and attitudes. These can be enhanced by sensible choices about the games to use.

How many games in a program? As a general rule, games should not be the dominant feature in programs. Only occasionally should a program be games only. Games do not have to be long. But a normal program could include two or three games.

As a program requires variety in its make-up, so do games need to be chosen in terms of variety.

There are three guidelines about including games. Broadly these are:

- use the boisterous type of game early in the program. Do not use this type at the end otherwise children will be leaving over-excited and scatter-brained
- use a sense-training, or knowledge type game somewhere in the middle to help break up long periods in the program
- use co-operative, circle, non-competitive games towards the end of the program

What are the types of games?

By putting games into groups we see clearly how diverse games are, and this helps us make better choices about the best place to use particular games in a program. Seven categories of games will be described. You will find examples of each of these later in this learning program.

1. Steam games

These are games in which everyone participates, played in or out of doors. They allow for strenuous activity, but are not body-contact in type. The games are 'all in/all the time' so if a person is 'caught' there is a means for the person to rejoin the game without delay. Such games are excellent in the early part of a program. They leave children 'huffing and puffing' and ready to sit down, or to move onto something quieter.

2. Circle games

These can be energetic to quiet in style. The circle provides the formation for the action. Elimination of players is avoided. (The formation of groups of children who have been eliminated from games ought to be avoided. They are missing involvement; misbehaviour can become a means for finding action again.)

3. Relay games

These are games for small groups (your club may be using sub-groupings as teams) in relay formation. A competitive spirit often accompanies such activities, consequently requiring care that rules are followed, and the children 'play fair'. The purpose of a relay may be training in a skill (for example hopping, bouncing a ball), or for fun (for example carrying water in a teaspoon). Remember that in a relay usually only one person in the team is active at any given time.

4. Team games

The club is formed into teams. The aim is to help members strive for their team, rather than for themselves only. Team games range from physically exuberant types to those requiring mental effort in co-operative form.

5. Sense training games

Games can be devised which will help children sharpen their senses. Concentration will be required either in seeing, listening, tasting, touching or smelling.

6. Quiet games

This is the opportunity for children to enjoy a different pace for a period. Some 'parlour games' are suitable. Play-acting games, which whilst needing some movement, are quieter in tone.

7. Wide games

The outdoors is the setting for these games. They are not to confused with 'steam', 'circle', 'team' or 'relay' games which could also be played outside. Rather, 'wide' games take place over broad terrain, and often involve stalking, hiding, seeking, running, breaking codes and carrying messages. Teams may be required. For older children such games can be played at night (if you know the site well). Generally speaking with the club age group, day time 'wide' games are recommended.

What guidelines are there for choosing and using games? Here are five pointers.

1. Variety as mentioned, but avoid the trap of only using a small selection of games. Keep the approach fresh. Only infrequently replay a familiar game that you know the children enjoy. Remember, too, that by changing the name and description of the action, you and the child's imagination have made a new game.

2. Use planning judgment so that games are chosen to enhance the overall program. Games should dovetail their mood and energy level with the other elements of the program.

3. Stress participation rather than competition. Avoid using prizes. It is more important for everybody to play than it is for someone to win. If your club has teams, and you use a points system, consider these ideas:
   - do not prolong a points tally beyond six meetings. Then start again.
   - give points for winning, but only if you also give points for the fairest team, the most enthusiastic team, and the team with the straightest line.

4. Choose games which are appropriate for the physical abilities and stamina of the children. Do not prolong games to the point where children are exhausted. Energy can be lost before enthusiasm. As a rule finish a game with children wanting more.

5. Boys and girls will be playing together. Choose games which are not 'body-attack' in type, in which aggression, stamina and physical strength are paramount. Rather 'body-tag' games are a better choice. These require agility, speed, quick moves, and simple touching on hands, shoulders or backs.

Much of the success or failure of a game in a program depends on whether the game has been introduced and explained accurately, and enthusiastically. Here are six pointers.

1. Explain the rules as simply as possible. Have these clear in your own mind as you have mentally 'walked through' the game beforehand.

2. Demonstrate the game by a brief tryout, so that everyone can become accustomed to its procedures. Explain further if necessary.

3. Commence the game. If a game goes awry, then it will not cure itself. Stop it, point out the problem, and restart. If foul play develops, stop the game, explain what you have seen, and start again. Show that you expect the rules to be followed.

4. If the game needs it, *you* revise the rules, or add a new rule.

5. Call for fast movement, keen attention, and straight lines. Congratulate the first team in line ready to begin. Make good order a fun challenge and self-discipline is developed.

6. Playing games is enjoyable. Add to the enjoyment by occasionally doing the unusual — sometimes use a whistle to start, sometimes call 'ready, set, go!' sometimes wave a Grand Prix flag, or sometimes say 'The game will start when I touch my right knee!'

Task

Begin practising these six points in introducing and conducting games. When you are ready, ask your mentor to observe a game you are conducting at a club meeting.

What games equipment is needed in a club? There are many games which require either no equipment, or minimal or improvised equipment. But the following items can be assembled over time, and will have many uses. The equipment box can include balls (soccer size, plastic), plastic balls (tennis ball size), stocking balls (make these yourself), nurf balls, bean bags, batons, a home made cricket bat, quoits or rubber rings, skipping ropes, and ice-cream buckets. Plastic balls should be bought in sets, so that you have a set, all the same size, in the ratio of one ball for every six children. A ready supply of chalk will be useful, too. It is wise to store the equipment in a secure place, and only bring out what is needed for the evening program.

Task

Commence your own *Games Book*. Procure a ringed folder (you could use the back of your *Program Book*), and make partitions for each of the seven types of games, for example steam, team, quiet, etc. Then as you find games, or see them used elsewhere, write them into your *Games Book*. Keep adding to your collection as you discover new material. Put in the games on pages 60 and 61. Whenever you use a game from your collection, note its date, and any additional notes about rules or equipment. Show your mentor your *Games Book*. It will be a valuable resource.

Playing games safely. The aim is to have games which, at times, will be fast-moving and exuberant. Several precautions will help maintain safe conduct.

1. Ensure the playing space is uncluttered, chairs and forms cleared, and is not a 'walk through' area.

2. Ensure fair, clean play is the expected standard, and withdraw a child from a game if the child persists in unsafe behaviour.

3. Give discreet attention to any children whose enthusiasm and impetuosity are stronger than their reasoning. A hand on the shoulder can prevent hot-headed behaviour on many occasions.

4. Plan out in your mind beforehand, how you see the game running. Try to foresee any difficulties.

If children are knocked or fall, let them relax for a moment, but let them get back into things as soon as possible.

6 CRAFTS IN THE PROGRAM

Some children's clubs have been built around craft as the central activity. Other clubs will treat craft as a particular program element in a more diverse program.

What are the reasons for using craft activities? Here are five factors.

We use craft:

1. because children of club age like to make things, and use their creative abilities

2. because craft activity encourages the development of children's co-ordination, physical and mental growth

3. because it develops children's ability to visualise, and to satisfy their urge to experiment

4. because it provides an outlet for their active imagination

5. because it helps a child to discover answers to the 'Who am I?' question.

Beware the adult trap! As adults, we sometimes have expectations of children's ability to produce quality products, which are too high. Craft items need to be designed in broad terms, avoiding finicky detail. Although abilities may be limited because of age and experience, imaginations are not. The leader should look for and praise effort, enjoyment and creativity, not expecting highly polished outcomes.

Beware the trap! It is too easy to define craft as scissors, paper and paste activity. Children will be stimulated by activities which are challenging and appealing, and this will mean using a range of items, materials, tools and methods. Consider these four pointers.

1. Use a variety of approaches over time

2. Use crafts that will give children new experiences with different materials and tools, for example hammers, saws, or painting with varnish.

3. From time to time, use crafts that end up as simple toys for the children to play with, or to give away, for example paddleboats, puppets.

4. Use crafts that are designed to stimulate the imagination on the night, for example box sculptures, items that are necessary for the next activity or property making for play-acting mimes or skits.

Here is a checklist of *materials*.

Light garden wire	pine off-cuts	papier mâché
pegs	beads	poster paint
wood	felt	rocks
cardboard boxes — all sizes and shapes	paper plates	fabric
	hessian	particle board
polystyrene foam	cardboard	plastic raffia
leather	upholstery vinyl	clay
wool — yarn and lamb's wool	printer's ink — soluble	sand
		coloured card
aluminium foil	vegetables	plaster of Paris
drawing paper	plastic bottles — all sizes	driftwood pieces
cotton reels	candle-wax	string
cardboard tubes	condensed milk tins	soap
	tree pods, seeds, nuts	shells

Here is a list of *craft ideas*.
Masks, shields, animals, birds, vehicles, helicopters, aeroplanes, kites, mobiles, imaginative creatures, totems, racing cars, space station, miniature gardens, diorama models, marionettes, glove puppets, rod puppets, mask plaques, relief pictures, table mats, leather items, pottery, potato printing, lino cut printing, leaf/flower patterns, paper flowers, rug squares, doll's house furniture, peep hole theatre, candles, gadgets, puzzles, baskets, bird box, dog lead, picture frame, model Bible scenes, book, posters, banners, macrame, photography, cuttle fish carving, rhythm instruments.

Here is a list of *tools* appropriate for club aged children.
Hammers, saws, wood brace and bit, leather hole punch, leather stamps, scissors, brad-awl, gimlet, screwdriver, vice, pliers, file, clamp, sandpaper, hot wire foam cutter and glue.

Help and supervision are required.

What about cutting blades? Close supervision is required to teach children to use tools correctly and safely. Blades can be used (most materials would be pre-cut) with care. Blades need to be clean and sharp (blunt tools take much more effort to use) and covered (Stanley knife or modeller's blade knife, as examples.) Such tools are put away once children have used them.

Task
These three lists can be used as a prompt. Look through them from time to time in order to check:
- **are we using different materials?**
- **are we producing different types and styles of craft objects?**
- **are we using a range of tools?**

Describe to your mentor the crafts you have used over the last six meetings, and discuss the variety you have achieved.

How do you set up craft activities? Good planning is the secret. The preparations beforehand need to be thorough so that:

1. every child has materials

2. there are sufficient tools for each child to have opportunity, without long queues

3. there are sufficient work places or tables for each child to have workroom

4. there is enough adult supervision (resource persons, helpers, parents) so that progress is supervised, depending on the nature of the activity

5. the activity is tested out at home beforehand so that quantities and execution time are known

6. for messy crafts, the children use old shirts or cover-alls, and newspapers are spread on the floor

7. items which will take more than one meeting to complete, can have the child's name attached, and storage in a safe place provided.

Task

1. **Find a craft idea that the club has not used before (not necessarily a new idea, but new to the club.)**

2. **Make all the planning and preparation steps to use the activity in the club.**

3. **Conduct the activity, and invite your mentor to visit and see the children in action.**

4. **After the activity, discuss with your mentor your evaluation of the success of the craft activity. Was it appealing to the children? Was it challenging? Imagination stirring? Did they enjoy it? How well were the seven points put into action? Is there anything that you would do differently next time?**

7 SINGING IN THE CHILDREN'S CLUB

It is accepted that a children's club would use singing as part of its program, especially because of the club worship times. But singing can meet a broader function in the club. Consider these:

1. Singing builds a common bond. It helps the development of fellowship and comradeship.

2. It allows the expression of emotion. On the one hand, the 'finer' emotions of sensibility and empathy can be fostered, and on the other, the emotions of aggression can be diverted in songs which require action, energy and exuberance.

3. Singing allows the 'emotional climate' of the club to be softened or strengthened as need be.

4. Singing allows children to express themselves, not only as individuals, but as a group.

5. Singing provides spiritual stimulation

6. Singing will be discovered as 'good fun' and enjoyable, and will frequently give children ways for expressing their sense of humour, or their love of the ridiculous.

I suggest four steps for introducing singing to your club.

Step 1. Find a song-leader. This could be yourself or one of your assistants. The person does not have to be a musician, but simply one who enjoys singing, and has the ability, or potential, to lead children in informal singing. If the person can use an instrument (piano, piano accordian, banjo or guitar) then this can be an advantage, but it is not essential.

Step 2. Have an aim, over a series of meetings, to build a repertoire of songs. Teach one or two new songs each night, and revise one or two learnt previously. Start and finish the singing segment with songs the children know and enjoy. Have the words on charts, or O.H.P. slides, but repetitive phrase songs are easy to learn and printed words will not be needed.

Step 3. Seat the children in a close semi-circle, perhaps on carpet on the floor. The song-leader insists on quiet before commencement, and keeps eye contact with the children during the singing. The song-leader can beat time, but the main thing is to sing enthusiastically, and sweep the children along. Stress that singing does not require shouting. Good singing means loud or soft singing according to the nature of the song.

Step 4. A new song can be introduced by:

a. the leader singing the chorus or verse to listen to the tune
b. the children trying it through
c. correcting any segments
d. trying again, then moving to the next verse. Praise the children for progress that is achieved. If the song includes actions then incorporate these as soon as possible. Humorous and action songs are the key to raising children's interest in singing. When the enjoyment of that is found, then more melodic or meaningful songs can follow.

Some clubs lack a song-leader. In such cases, having songs recorded on tape will be a help. Church resource centres will have worship songs available, but for others you may have them recorded by a friendly musician. Take note, however, that you should record a musician with two or three singers, singing at the appropriate tempo for the song. This will be suitable for children to accompany. If the recording is of an instrument only the children will find it hard to keep in time.

Five categories of songs are suggested as suitable in a club.

1 Action songs

Children find much enjoyment in these. They are good fun, and the physical activity and co-ordination required are appropriate for the age-group.

Some songs of the action type are: John Brown's baby; One finger, one thumb; Chester; Three wood pigeons; McNamara's band; Black Crow Indian; Father Abraham; Put on love everyday; The grand old Duke of York.

2 Fun and nonsense songs

Children have a sense of the ridiculous. These songs express humour, and give them the opportunity to sing nonsense words. Included with these would be non-songs such as 'Yells' or 'The Lion Hunt' or 'The King with the Terrible Temper'.

Some songs of the fun and nonsense type are: One man went to mow; Old MacDonald had a farm; Quartermaster's store; She'll be coming round the mountain; Clementine; Found a peanut; There's a hole in my bucket; Bill Groggin's goat; Bold Tommy Payne.

3 Folk Songs

These songs, as their background is explained, expand the child's world. Folk songs help children feel in touch with other peoples and their histories. Many of these are melodic songs that do not have to be sung loudly. They are spiritually stimulating in many cases.

A selection of suitable folk songs would include: The old bark hut; Waltzing Matilda; The springtime it brings on the shearing; Click go the shears; Drover's dream; Bound for South Australia (Australia); Looky, looky, yonder; Deep blue sea; Skip to my Lou; Pick a bale o'cotton (U.S.A.); Red River Valley; Alouette (Canada); Billy Boy (England); And everyone 'neath the vine and fig tree (Israel); Now is the hour (New Zealand).

4 Rounds and harmony songs

Once the club has gained some experience in singing, and knows the enjoyment to be found,

then rounds will add a new dimension. Rounds create beautiful sounds if the aim is to sing melodically and not loudly. Ask children to listen as well as sing. It is a help to have a leader for each part.

Several songs of this type are: Campfire's burning; Row, row your boat; Kookaburra; Frère Jacques; O, how lovely is the evening.

5 Spirituals and Sacred Songs

These are songs to use toward the end of a sing-song, or toward the end of a camp-fire if the club is in camp. They are songs with a special mood. To these would be added the special worship songs that the children use in Sunday school and church worship.

A selection of spirituals and sacred songs: Jacob's ladder; Kumbayah; Rock my soul; Michael; Swing low, sweet chariot; I got a robe; O Mary, don't you weep; O come and go with me; Let my people go.

Where can you find these songs, and others like them? The best advice is 'Keep your eyes open' as you visit music stores, Scout outdoor centres, Girl Guide shops, Church bookstores with children's ministry resources, or bookstores offering school curriculum materials. Schools broadcast books will be a source.

Task

1. Choose a song that you want the club to learn and enjoy, and that you could lead.
2. Teach the song at one meeting time.
3. Ask your mentor to visit the club when your particular song is included again.
4. Ask your mentor to give you feedback on whatever area you choose, for example eye contact, control of the singing activity, involving the children, etc.
The important thing is to have your club finding enjoyment and comradeship as the children sing together.

---

8 STORIES

Everybody loves a good story. For children, stories will meet particular needs, and contribute to their mental and spiritual development.

What do stories do for children? Here are four aspects:

- stories enlist the lively imagination of children
- stories enlarge the child's world

- stories convey values, principles and spiritual truths, but in a concrete form
- stories provide interest, excitement, enjoyment, tension and involvement.

There are some key points to note about using stories. The first is that children are 'concrete' thinkers. The ability to think in concepts and principles has not yet developed. For most this will not happen until the years of adolescence. For example, they will not be thinking about 'justice' as a philosophical concept, but they will know what 'fair play' means in a story about a ball team, or a school class. Children will relate to people, events, happenings, places, adventures and episodes which can be imagined in the mind through a story.

The second is that some styles of stories may not be attractive, or may not be wisely used with this age group. For example, stories of romantic love or fairies will not be popular. Stories of a maudlin type, or filled with ghosts, or horrible creatures, should generally be avoided because of the over-stimulation that these may cause, especially when children are going home in the dark, close to bedtime.

Third, the stories chosen must appeal to the story teller. If you do not feel at ease with the story, then do not use it.

There are numerous sources of suitable stories. The Bible will be the first source for church club leaders. A Bible story, however, needs as much preparation and skill for its telling as any other story. Finding a story in the Bible is no guarantee that it will be accepted in its telling, unless we follow some guidelines and prepare accordingly.

There are many other sources such as children's story books, newspaper stories, magazines, real life stories, incidents from your own experience and so on. A story teller may take the barest outline of a plot and make it into an appealing account with some careful preparation. The stories we will want to work on will be those that convey moral and spiritual values arising from the Christian way.

In preparing and rehearsing a story, these points will be useful:

- choose a story you like, and that you sense will appeal to your group
- read the story to yourself, and build images of the places and the people, and establish the thought line of the plot
- make brief notes on a card (which you can clip in your program book)
- tell the story out loud, to yourself, at home

- prepare especially carefully the beginning and the ending. The ending should be clear, concise and pointed.

What is the form of a story? Well told stories build to a climax. The punchline is not given in the introduction, rather the story builds towards its climax and conclusion. The hero story, for example, traditionally follows a certain pattern. It is wise to recognise this pattern and use it; this will avoid doing two things.

- First, putting the climax in the wrong place, and
- Second, spoiling the ending by moralising.

The hero story will conform to this pattern. Whether you think of the encounter between David and Goliath, or the whole ministry of Jesus, or of a story of a dramatic rescue at night by the Flying Doctor, here is the pattern of the hero story.

- The person recognises their challenge, their call, their purpose, ideals and aims.
- The person undertakes the challenge.
- The person encounters tough experiences, trying tests, and temptations which come upon them as attempts are made to meet the challenges.
- The person's struggles continue.
- There seem to be insurmountable odds, and the added battle of fighting against temptations to give up, and withdraw.
- Then, either the person dies beneath the pressures but victory is won by those who follow, or the person becomes victorious and accomplishes the mission, challenge or call.

Stories of people with moral and spiritual integrity, who put their ideals and faith into action, whether they lived to see the final result or not, are powerful stories. The hero pattern can be seen in an episode of life, some special task or mission, or it can be seen as the framework for the whole of a hero's life. Either way, the hero and his or her struggles will be vibrant material.

When telling a story, put these points into practice:

- be sure that the children are seated comfortably, close to you, but not behind you
- establish eye contact with them
- use a good opening that gets their interest right away
- stick to your plan, as you have rehearsed it
- speak simply, clearly, naturally, and not too quickly
- use gestures
- particular characters may need special voices

- if needed, show pictures or objects
- if you think it is necessary to state the moral, or purpose of the story, do this well before the climax
- when you reach the climax of the story, then finish. This is why rehearsing the ending is important, so that you know how to finish well.

Do I use visual aids? Sometimes these will be beneficial. Children always like to see things. But if the setting of the story, or the people and their clothing, or other matters are hard to describe, then illustrations may help. Pictures need to be large enough. Draw them simply yourself, or enlarge them by overhead projector transparencies.

Should I read the story? On occasions this is appropriate, especially if the language of the story is lyrical, or perhaps ludicrous. Lively reading with frequent eye contact around the group is essential.

Story telling is an area of club programs that can become more meaningful through practice and experience, and being prepared to work at it. The rewards are considerable as you discover the interest and enjoyment the children find in well told stories.

Task

When you are ready, invite your mentor to visit the club on an occasion when you are telling a story. Ask for feedback in areas important to you, for example was there rapport with the children? Did the story flow well? Did the moral point of the story come through without moralising? Were the beginning and ending effective?

9 DISCOVERY TIME

The child's world is expanding through these years of primary school. Children are curious and interested in new things. Why not captivate their fascination for discovering new things by frequently building in a 'discovery time' in programs?

These can be short segments when time is given to simple experiments, looking at a collection that someone has brought, looking at photographs on a theme, or hearing about someone's hobby. The purpose is to expand children's horizons, and arouse their curiosity further.

Here is a starter list of ideas. Keep eyes and ears open. There are people in the congregation who could bring, or demonstrate, or display topics which would interest children. Starter ideas for discovery times could include these: iron filings, card and a magnet; gowns worn by people last century; jewelry making with gem stones; tools used by a woodcarver; what a minister uses when taking Holy Communion to sick people; old books or old children's picture books; building model trains; clock and watch collection; a display of first day covers; restoring a vintage car; writing with a quill; maps — old and new; compasses; what does SCUBA mean?; how a marionette works; rocks; core samples from a drilling operation; unusual souvenirs.

There are some advantages in using visiting speakers from time to time, but there are also some preparatory steps required so that the visit is productive. The leader will need to check these matters, to ensure:

1. that the speaker is approached well ahead, and has the date booked

2. that the speaker knows when and where to come, time of arrival, and length of time given for his/her segment

3. that the speaker is aware of:
   a. the time limit (8–10 minutes)

   b. the age of the children

   c. the attention span of such children

   d. the limited field to be covered on this occasion

   e. what items to bring for display

   f. and to ask, and arrange to supply, items such as chalkboard, O.H.P., display boards or tables as needed

   g. and to check whether the speaker will invite questions.

The leader needs to check with the speaker one week prior to ensure all is in hand.

Why check all these matters beforehand? Experience shows that many adults, who are enthralled by their hobby or interest, may not be trained to speak to children, and may easily fall into the traps of speaking for too long, trying to cover too much, or speaking at a level deeper than necessary. If the leader with diplomatic preparation beforehand can assist the visitor to meet these criteria, then the purpose of widening children's horizons can be achieved without boredom.

Having a visiting speaker also affords the club with a training purpose. The speaker needs to be introduced and thanked. These are tasks for children to do. They will need some guidance from you so that they are equipped to fulfil their tasks.

10 DRESS-UP PROGRAMS

Several times a year a 'dress-up' night can be featured. A theme can be adopted, to which the costuming relates, and then the segments of the program are devised on the lines of the theme. A special supper can be included. The accent of make-believe can be more strongly made.

It is essential, however, for parents to be given guidance about a 'dress-up' program by way of written and spoken communications. A 'dress-up' night is not a competition night for the best costume. It is not an expensive episode where parents are expected to make special costumes, or hire costumes. The stress should be on:

- choosing a theme which can be simply expressed in costumes
- emphasising costuming which can be put together from items at home
- requiring children to create costume items themselves.

Other important factors are:

- leaders dress up too; everybody joins in the fun
- the meeting place is decorated according to the theme, to add interest
- the supper relates to the theme.

Exciting 'dress-up' programs can be designed around ideas such as:

international	holiday
Disneyland	journey into space
country fair	pioneers
clowns and circus	Swiss Family Robinson
knights and maidens of old	swaggies — Waltzing Matilda
Olympic Games	the zoo

The content of the program will not be much different from the usual. The theme runs through all the segments. There may be more games than usual, but discovery time, story and worship aim to provide learning and faith stimulating material. The best method for devising a 'dress-up' program is for the leadership team to begin planning a long way ahead, and to use one or two of their planning meetings to let their imaginations roam, working out the content.

11 WORSHIP AND PRAYERS

A significant training ground in the use of the Bible and in the practice of prayer is found in the children's club. The worship in the club will be one in which Bible reading and prayer are fostered and practised. The ways for children to participate in the activities of worship need to be discovered and utilised by the club leader.

Such worship activity belongs to program planning and conduct. But it also needs to be seen from the viewpoint of fostering faith development. Thus detailed attention to worship in the club is to be found in Chapter 7 'Pastoral care and faith development in a children's club'. Similarly the program on 'Outreach' includes material which impinges on program planning and conduct.

12 OPENING AND CLOSING MEETINGS

There are no set ways in which a club should open and close its meetings. There are advantages in formulating one or two patterns for opening and closing which become well known to the children.

Opening suggestions:

Begin by standing in a circle. Newcomers can be introduced. Announcements about the program can be made. The club may have its own regular prayer, which is read, or said together.

Closing suggestions:

Use the circle formation. After reminders, sing together 'We are going home with God'. Or a sentence prayer, which can be often used, and spoken together: 'We are glad that we have been together, we are glad that when we go, you go with us. Amen'.

Task

Here are three examples taken from three different leaders' program notes. As you read them ask yourself these questions:

1. **Could I run this program from the information given?**

2. **Could an assistant run this program if I could not attend?**

3. **What else do I need to do to improve my program planning skills?**

Read the examples and share your comments with your mentor.

Example 1

Date: 30th March

Time	Program Segment	Leader	Equipment
7.00	Opening in a circle Welcome, introductions	Jill	
7.05	Games: Kangaroo Hop	Jim	
	Touch something	Jill	
7.20	Discovery time: Mr Malloy will bring collection of old and other language Bibles — inc. miniscule New Testament		3 tables
7.30	Team game: Spokes	Pat	4 bean bags
7.40	Craft: Critter making with natural materials	All	Pods, eyes gum nuts
8.10	Quiet game: Sleeping Pirate	Pat	Blindfold bean bag
8.20	Story: The girl who wanted a Bible — how the Bible Soc. began	Jill	
8.30	Worship: song prayer	Pat's group Jim's group	Books
8.35	Closing in circle Shared blessing		

Example 2

Program for Kid's Club

30th March	Make critters from natural materials
6th April	First Aid — St John Ambulance
20th April	Devotional program

Example 3

Kid's Club Program 4th May
Games
Craft: making pendants with plaster
Story
Closing worship

Comments:

1. Example 2 gives the type of notes a leader would make in the term program (Part 2) sheets of the leader's *Program Book*. The entries do not have enough information for a substitute leader to run an evening program.
2. Example 3 gives an interim indication of what the program may become. Not enough information yet.
3. Example 1 provides a detailed outline. The program can be conducted with some flexibility. If need be, a game can be dropped out if the visitor or the craft take longer than planned, especially if the children are enthused and want more. The program is clearly thought through. Another person, in an emergency, could step in and run the program.

13 USEFUL RESOURCES

When opportunities come, browse in bookshops with displays on children's work, or school curriculum resources, or children's hobbies and activities. Your church book store will have materials on children's ministry and activities. Ideas may be discovered in many places by leaders who have eyes to see.

Two useful books on program planning are:
Kids Club, (a children and your church strategy paper), Uniting Church Press, Melbourne, 1989.

Cub Scout Leaders Handbook (The Scout Association of Australia, in conjunction with Horwitz Grahame Pty Ltd, 1988.) This title would be available at a Scout Outdoor Centre.

14 THE CLUB LEADER CONDUCTS CLUB PROGRAMS

This chapter has concentrated on planning and conducting club programs. A full, well run program, will assist your work in two special ways:

- children will keep on coming because of the interest, enjoyment and fun of belonging
- discipline problems will be minimised if the program is lively and challenging.

So the club leader will want to keep checking the content of programs for their balance, interest and challenge. The club leader will work at planning by looking ahead, so improving the relationship of the club activities to other events in the church's life. The club leader will also recognise the skills to be developed in leading children, especially in the program of the club. As with most skills, learning comes with practice. High skill comes through experience, and trying to learn through reflection, accepting feedback, and having our eyes set on standards to achieve. The idea of this self-assessment is so that you can assess the progress you have made in developing and using the skills of program leadership. Can you do better now than when you started?

SELF-ASSESSMENT

When you have completed the tasks outlined in this program, then you will be ready for this assessment activity with the aid of your mentor.

It is a joint activity, with conversation, through which your mentor will endorse the completion of the tasks. The mentor will be looking at your activities in the club, and helping you assess whether you have performed the various functions according to the suggested standards.

Levels of performance: place an 'X' in the appropriate box. If, because of special circumstances, a component was not applicable, or impossible to execute, an 'X' may be placed in the 'not applicable' box. All items should receive either a n/a, good or excellent response. If any item receives a none, poor or fair response then you and the mentor will need to determine what additional activities are required in order to complete that component. It may mean having more practice, and then inviting your mentor to observe you and the club in action again. The aim is a personal one — to be able to lead children's club programs well.

	N/A	None	Poor	Fair	Good	Excellent
1 As leader, I use						
a. a program book	☐	☐	☐	☐	☐	☐
b. an annual planner	☐	☐	☐	☐	☐	☐
c. term by term sheets	☐	☐	☐	☐	☐	☐
d. individual program sheets completed in detail.	☐	☐	☐	☐	☐	☐
2. As leader, I have conducted three programs that						
a. started on time	☐	☐	☐	☐	☐	☐
b. finished on time	☐	☐	☐	☐	☐	☐
c. used a detailed program plan	☐	☐	☐	☐	☐	☐
d. contained a variety of elements	☐	☐	☐	☐	☐	☐
e. were structured and balanced	☐	☐	☐	☐	☐	☐

	N/A	None	Poor	Fair	Good	Excellent
f. used a simple 'beginning' format	☐	☐	☐	☐	☐	☐
g. used a simple 'ending' format.	☐	☐	☐	☐	☐	☐
3 As leader, I have conducted games over a period of six meetings using at least four of these types						
a. steam	☐	☐	☐	☐	☐	☐
b. circle	☐	☐	☐	☐	☐	☐
c. relay	☐	☐	☐	☐	☐	☐
d. team	☐	☐	☐	☐	☐	☐
e. sense training	☐	☐	☐	☐	☐	☐
f. quiet	☐	☐	☐	☐	☐	☐
g. wide.	☐	☐	☐	☐	☐	☐
4 As leader, I conduct games by						
a. explaining rules clearly	☐	☐	☐	☐	☐	☐
b. using practice runs	☐	☐	☐	☐	☐	☐
c. stopping infringements.	☐	☐	☐	☐	☐	☐
5 As leader, I conduct activities, games, etc. safely by						
a. clearing the space	☐	☐	☐	☐	☐	☐
b. setting boundaries	☐	☐	☐	☐	☐	☐
c. defining rules	☐	☐	☐	☐	☐	☐
d. supervising over-zealous children	☐	☐	☐	☐	☐	☐
e. stopping unfair play.	☐	☐	☐	☐	☐	☐
6 As leader, I conduct craft activities, which over six meetings display at least						
a. two craft methods	☐	☐	☐	☐	☐	☐
b. two main craft materials	☐	☐	☐	☐	☐	☐

Rating columns: N/A | None | Poor | Fair | Good | Excellent

c. different tools, instruments. ☐☐☐☐☐☐

7 As leader, I conduct craft activities on each occasion, with
a. sufficient materials for each child ☐☐☐☐☐☐

b. work space for each child ☐☐☐☐☐☐

c. sufficient equipment for each child to have fair use. ☐☐☐☐☐☐

8 As leader, I conduct craft activities which, in each case, were tested beforehand in regard to
a. time for completion ☐☐☐☐☐☐

b. suitability of materials ☐☐☐☐☐☐

c. assessment of suitable tools. ☐☐☐☐☐☐

9 As leader, I conduct singing by
a. leading or ☐☐☐☐☐☐

b. by delegating of song leading. ☐☐☐☐☐☐

10 As leader, I include songs of at least three of these categories in a period of six meetings
a. action ☐☐☐☐☐☐

b. fun and nonsense ☐☐☐☐☐☐

c. folk ☐☐☐☐☐☐

d. rounds and harmony ☐☐☐☐☐☐

e. spiritual and sacred. ☐☐☐☐☐☐

11 As leader, I tell stories on at least three occasions in a period of six meetings, which
a. support Christian values ☐☐☐☐☐☐

b. relate Bible truths or ☐☐☐☐☐☐

c. are Bible stories. ☐☐☐☐☐☐

12 As leader, I tell stories on each occasion, which
a. are suitable for 'concrete' thinkers ☐☐☐☐☐☐

b. use simple language ☐☐☐☐☐☐

c. avoid moralising ☐☐☐☐☐☐

d. use lively voice, tone. ☐☐☐☐☐☐

13 As leader, I tell stories on each occasion, by
a. seating the children comfortably ☐☐☐☐☐☐

b. quietening children ☐☐☐☐☐☐

c. using eye contact ☐☐☐☐☐☐

d. speaking directly to children. ☐☐☐☐☐☐

14 As leader, in telling stories on three occasions, I have a:
a. clear, interesting beginning ☐☐☐☐☐☐

b. crisp, well prepared ending ☐☐☐☐☐☐

c. clear grasp of story line. ☐☐☐☐☐☐

15 Over a period of eight meetings I, as leader, have included at least three discovery times. ☐☐☐☐☐☐

16 When using a visiting speaker, as leader I have, on each occasion,
a. booked speaker early ☐☐☐☐☐☐

b. checked speaker week prior ☐☐☐☐☐☐

59

	N/A	None	Poor	Fair	Good	Excellent
c. indicated speaker's time	☐	☐	☐	☐	☐	☐
d. checked speaker's knowledge of child audience	☐	☐	☐	☐	☐	
e. arranged for child to introduce speaker	☐	☐	☐	☐	☐	
f. arranged for child to thank speaker.	☐	☐	☐	☐	☐	

Mentor's endorsement

I declare that (leader's name) ....
has completed the self-assessment tasks of this
learning program with good or excellent
markings.

Signed............................. (mentor)..............(date)

Games suitable for a church children's club

Steam games

1. Kangaroo hop

The children run free in the playing space. One person is 'kangaroo' and this child must hop with ankles together. Any other person touched by 'kangaroo' must also hop. Any child hopping has the power, by touching, to make others hop too. When all are hopping, choose a new 'kangaroo', and begin again.

2. Police cars

Two children are chosen to be police officers. A fairly large corner area of the playing space is marked off with a chalk line, and this is called the police car, which is guarded by one of the police officers (who must stay inside the chalk line). The other police officer chases the robbers (the rest of the club). If the police officer touches a robber, then the robber goes into the police car (behind the chalk line) and must stay there unless touched by a free robber, to be freed. The police officer in the car, however, can reach out and touch anybody coming close, or any person trying to free a robber. Restart the game if all the robbers are caught!

Circle games

3. Circle tunnel ball

The club members form a circle. Several balls (can be of different sizes) are put on the move from child to child, backwards beneath legs. When the whistle is blown, the children jump to turn and send the balls in the opposite direction.

4. String circle

A circle of string with a curtain ring threaded on it, is placed behind the backs of the children, who are formed in a circle. One child stands in the centre with eyes closed. The ring is passed from hand to hand, and when the child opens his/her eyes, and while the leader counts to three, the child tries to guess where the ring is. If the guess is correct, the two children change places. Let a child be in the centre for no more than two guesses, so that a number can have the opportunity.

Relay games

5. Hole to hole play

The children are in teams in relay formation. Two circles are drawn with chalk on the floor in front of each team — one about six paces out, the other ten. In one circle is a quoit or beanbag. The game requires the children in turn, to run out and shift the object from one circle to the other.

6. Bandy knees

The children are in relay formation. The team members have to jump with a ball between their knees — up and back. Chalk a mark about eight paces in front of each team. If a ball is dropped, the child has to run back to the start, or to the line, to complete the journey.

Team games

7. 'Undressing' game

The children are lined up in their teams. Each team has a length of rope tied into a circle. The ropes are placed at the feet of the first child in each line. On the command, the child steps into the rope, pulls it up and over, and hands it to the next child. The first team to finish and to return their rope to the front of the line, wins.

8. Paper chains

Each team has several copies of old newspapers, and a large supply of ordinary pins. The team making the longest unbroken chain of paper, supported at each end, and not touching the floor, wins. The time limit should be long enough for there to be a chance for a break in the chains, needing repair.

Sense training games

9. Colour cards

Set up a line of cards, coloured differently. A red card might be black on the back. A blue card might be yellow on the back, and so on. Use about six cards. Let children look at the cards, then they turn around, whilst the leader alters the set by turning one or two cards around. The children face the cards, and put their hands up if they can name the changes.

10. Washing display

Hang a line across the room, with ten different objects hung by string, with each covered by a plastic garbage bag. The children are not allowed to look, but by feeling inside the bags they try to identify the items and memorise the list without calling out. They then write down all those they can remember.

Quiet games

11. Secret agent

The secret agent sits on a chair guarding very confidential documents (a sheet of paper on the floor under the chair). It is night time so the agent is blindfolded. The children are in two lines on opposite sides of the playing space. They are the spies, and they must remain absolutely quiet and still. The leader chooses one spy to come, by pointing. The spy attempts to creep to the secret document in order to tear off a small portion (it is much too dangerous to take the whole document). If the spy can tear off a piece, and get back to his/her place without the secret agent hearing, then he/she wins a point for the team. The secret agent can dismiss a spy by pointing directly at him/her. The spy must then return to their place and the leader chooses a spy from the other team.

12. Count the seconds

The children stand anywhere on the playing space, with heads downturned and eyes closed. The leader announces the task — to guess how long half a minute is. The leader will say 'go' and watch the second hand. When children think that thirty seconds have passed they put up their hands. The leader notes which children were closest.

Wide game

13. Kit kan

This is a game to be played outdoors, preferably in a place where there are trees and bushes for hiding. The 'kan' is an empty fruit tin. One person is the keeper of the kan. The children conceal themselves not *too* far away from the kan. The keeper tries to spot the enemy. When he/she sees one, then the keeper runs back to the kan and calls 'kan, kan, Tim', and Tim must then come and stand by the kan. The keeper goes out again, until three are captured. Then a new keeper can be chosen. Meanwhile the enemy can attempt to creep up, especially when the keeper's back is turned. If the enemy can, they can rush the kan whilst the keeper is searching. They attempt to beat the keeper back to the kan. If they can kick the kan, and call 'Kan, Kan free', then the captured ones are freed, and they can hide again, and the keeper has to stay on until he/she can capture three more.

Program Sheet . . . Children's Club

Date:

Theme:

Team available: Team not available:

Time	Activity	Leader	Equipment

Birthdays:

Attendance: No. in attendance ....

    Out of total membership ....

Announcements: About next meeting ....

    About church activities:

Personal notes:

Chapter 7

Pastoral care and faith development

Children learn, develop and grow in their faith through the people they are with. Adults whom they respect and whose company they enjoy will have a high impact on children's faith development.

Let us mention seven factors that encourage faith development in children, before we look at some of the practical tasks in this learning program.

1 SEVEN FACTORS TO ENCOURAGE CHILDREN'S FAITH DEVELOPMENT

First, we acknowledge God's love which surrounds, covers and upholds us, and which seeks our response and commitment. God draws us to himself. It is his desire that we should be 'at home' in his presence. God as Creator, God in Jesus Christ, and God in the Spirit, seek to enfold us, and foster our growth. It is in that faith that we recognise that God is at work in the children we meet at children's club. Their development in the faith is the good Lord's concern. Our work with children is in response to the Lord's work in us all, drawing us to himself.

Secondly, children's faith development will be encouraged by the personal care, interest and friendship which they receive from Christian people. You and your assistants have a vital role here. As you show that each child matters to you, and as you affirm each one, you will encourage their spiritual growth. They will learn about caring from you.

This is why discipline and pastoral care are linked. Fair treatment and belief in the value and abilities of each child are important factors. As leader, you may well teach children how to love and care in Christ's name, because that is the way you treat children.

Thirdly, children need to belong, and know that they belong, to the community of faith. You will aid their spiritual development by:

- doing all you can to have children participate in the congregational life of the community of faith, especially worship
- doing all you can to move the congregation to embrace these children and their families in the community of faith
- doing all you can to help these children experience the special feeling of belonging to 'the people of Jesus'.

Fourthly, their faith development will be fostered as you model your own Christian life amongst children. As you witness in your own simple words why you follow and serve Jesus as the Lord of your life, you are helping children see the evidence of Christian commitment. All the better if children see that your Christian service is gladly given and joyful in nature. As we know children respond to enthusiasm.

Fifthly, you will foster the development of their faith as you pray, and give opportunity for children to pray, in the life of the club. You will encourage them in their individual prayer life, but more clearly in the club, you will involve them in corporate activities that lead to prayers together.

Sixthly, as you use the Bible in the club, you will foster their faith development in several ways. You will help them realise that the story of God's dealings with people, especially in Jesus, continues to our day. As your program allows children to work with the Bible in story, drama and creative activity, you will involve their thinking and feeling abilities. As you encourage personal use of the Bible at home, you will underline both the individual and community value which the Bible has to Christians. God will meet the children through Bible use.

Seventh, children's faith development will be encouraged as you make opportunities for children to talk about faith ideas and to speak their understandings out loud. Growth occurs through the processes of involvement. Play-acting, dramatising, painting, miming, problem-solving and interpreting in their own terms are all ways for children to work with matters of the Christian faith. Such involvement fosters faith development.

These seven factors provide an overview of faith development processes. There is always an element of mystery about human development, and especially spiritual growth. We work in faith knowing that for children their club leaders can be significant people who aid growth in their faith. So we turn to some of the practical matters of club leadership that will foster spiritual growth.

Task

This is a reading task. Procure a copy of Iris V. Cully, _Christian Child Development_ (Melbourne: The Joint Board of Christian Education, 1979.) In particular, read Chapter 5 on 'Religious Development'. Read this chapter while you are working on other parts of this program. You will find helpful material in other chapters too. Consider what you have read and discuss insights you have gained which broaden your understanding of children's faith development. Write down three points to share with your mentor.

2 PASTORAL CARE

Pastoral care is shown to children and their families in several ways. The leaders do all they can to know individual children. This means knowing particularly their interests, hobbies and pastimes. Remembering their birthdays and acknowledging special events in their lives are important factors.

This is important for every child, but especially so for some particular children. These are the children who do not necessarily shine out above the others. The reticent, the backward, the overweight, the worldly-poor, and those with low self-esteem will benefit from your friendly attention and care.

What are the important factors in the pastoral care of children in a club? Here are five important points:

- the leader knows the child by name
- the leader knows where the child lives and has called on the child at home at least once in the past twelve months
- the leader knows about the child's interests and hobbies, and can engage in conversation with each child
- the leader knows the child's parents
- the leader respects the child as a young Christian, and can converse in appropriate ways about belonging to the community of faith.

Before, during, and after meetings, at church events, at Sunday school and in occasional visits to children's homes, the leader builds relationships of friendship and interest with individuals. The child knows that he or she matters to the leader. It is on the foundation of knowledge and friendship that the leader will be able to act in Christian care when any crisis strikes a child and his or her family. It is Christian care in the ordinary which may allow for the exercise of Christian care in the extraordinary.

Task

This is a personal exercise. Look through the club roll. Can you picture each child? Can you tell yourself one thing about each child's interests, sports, hobbies, or school? Can you picture the house each child lives in? Does this exercise present you with a child's name where you sense you need to know the child better?

3 DISCIPLINE, ORDER AND PASTORAL CARE

These aspects of a club are closely related. A club will not be an effective centre for caring relationships if there is not good order, and an atmosphere that encourages self-discipline. Establishing good order will take time and effort.

Here are ten basic steps to take to establish good order.

1. Have a well-filled, busy program with variety. Do not be fearful of noise at the right time. Have ways in which energy and excitement can be used up to lead into quieter activities.

2. Learn children's names as soon as possible.

3. Set reasonable rules and enforce them consistently.

4. Believe in yourself, and your leadership of the club.

5. Praise and affirm individual children in personal ways.

6. Praise and affirm the club when good order and quick responses are forthcoming.

7. Show that you expect good behaviour and that you believe children can give it.

8. Show that you are fair and firm.

9. Take a team approach by ensuring that supervision is shared. Leaders who are not involved in a program segment should remain active in support.

10. Go back to point 1! Effective programming is the first essential in a self-disciplined club. The second essential is firm but fair leadership from leaders who love the children in Christ's name.

Misbehaviour

What about misbehaviour, and how to deal with it? Some children will try the leaders' patience. There are times when the general mood of the club tends towards being unco-operative. This may be simply the result of the weather. For example, tiring sultry weather may leave children lethargic, or windy stormy weather may cause children to be skitty and fractious.

Some individual children, however, may be disruptive or anti-social in their actions in the club. A way to approach these difficulties is by assuming that 'bad behaviour always means something'. Although the reasons are not clear, especially to the child, misbehaviour occurs for some reason. In those situations we should be asking ourselves:

Does this child need
- more individual attention
- more activity
- to succeed in something
- to know what he/she can do well
- affirmation, respect and love
- to learn the limits, and how to respect them?

Misbehaviour may be a claim for attention and time, but leaves the child open to rejection. Leaders need to learn how to reject the misbehaviour but not the child.

Here are ten ideas about dealing with misbehaviour in a club.

1. Show that certain rules exist for the good of everybody. Explain them and reinforce them.

2. Check violations of rules. This is particularly important in games. Sometimes misconduct is caused through exuberance and unthinking actions. To be told to sit out the activity may be sufficient checking in many cases.

3. The reprimanding of a child should happen away from the group. Try to use approaches that will engage the child's reasoning about what the misconduct was, what effect it had on others, and what should now be done.

Here is a set of questions which could be asked of the child. There is a type of transaction which this approach to misconduct could take.

Question: 'What did you do?'
Answer: (The child is required to describe what he/she has been doing.)

Question: 'Is what you have been doing helping your group, or the club?'
Answer: (The Child is required to describe what effect his/her conduct has had on others.)

Question: 'What could you do which is different? You tell me another way in which you could behave.'
Answer: (The child must attempt to do this. The leader can make suggestions as well.)

Question: 'What have you decided to do? You tell me what choice you have made.'
Answer: (The child makes a commitment, which the leader will expect to be followed.)

If misconduct occurs again, the same process occurs, with the leader expecting fulfilment of the child's commitment. Self-discipline comes through accepting personal obligations. Reprimands of this type, with the stress on personal application of thought, and naming of a commitment, are more effective than loud reprimands given publicly.

4. Consider two traps for leaders. The first is to overreact when confronted with misbehaviour, and to make punishment more severe than necessary. The other is to make threats that cannot be carried out. If you make a threat you must be ready to proceed with it. If a child persists in misbehaving after several warnings, and you have threatened to take the child home, then you must act on your threat. In other words, avoid threats such as 'I'll knock your block off!' Threats need to be realistic, enforceable, and represent a loss of some desirable activity as far as the child is concerned.

5. Using a team points reward system for a period can be a way of showing approval for appropriate, community-oriented behaviour. By the removal of points for disruptive conduct then the message is clear. Such reward systems should not be extended beyond six meetings, certainly not for a term, or a year. After six meetings, declare the winning team; then, if desired, start a new competition.

6. If a particular child is frequently disruptive, then the leaders as a team can plan a method for coping. This is anticipation, looking for the signs and then having an unobtrusive plan to help the child stay within the limits. Sometimes this misconduct will appear in games. A hand on the shoulder may be the reminder and will quieten the child before the activity is disrupted. Ways need to be devised for affirming the child and reinforcing and applauding approved behaviour.

7. Always be impartial, just and fair. Show that you expect co-operative behaviour (because the club is a community) and that you know the children can give it. Do not be afraid to show that you are disappointed with disruptive conduct, but be quick to praise, smile, affirm and sincerely congratulate the club for good order.

8. Recognise that learning how to control a club effectively, and help children develop self-discipline, is a long term task. The exercise of personal leadership is required, as well as personal and pastoral attention to each member.

9. Demeaning, sarcastic or discrediting comments are not productive. Expressed disappointment or controlled anger are not out of place, providing you can quickly turn to affirmation and praise.

10. Children grow when they can be decision-makers. Involve children in rule-making, say at the beginning of a new term, or when the rules need to be restated. Keep the rules few, simple and concise, Perhaps two or three children will print them on a poster.

Task

Reflection: **Have any of these ten ideas given you something new to consider? For example, have you tried ways of requiring a frequently disruptive child to describe his/her behaviour to you, and then telling you what he/she must do now? Discuss with your mentor ways you have found for effectively improving the control and building the self-discipline of members.**

4 MODELLING THE CHRISTIAN LIFE

Ask an adult Christian about their memories of childhood, and of the people who influenced them. The stories of people arise. 'I remember ---, she was my Sunday school teacher'. It also becomes clear that we find it easier to remember the persons who influenced us, rather than the facts they taught us. Adult Christians in any generation who care for children, give them time, and express personal interest in them, are significant people for their faith development.

Lawrence O. Richards in *A Theology of Christian Education* (Grand Rapids: Zondervan, 1975) identified seven factors in the modelling process. The child observes the leader. But as the leader also discloses his or her beliefs, values and faith, the child begins to recognise the ideals this person holds.

The modelling process will occur where:

- children have frequent, long term contact with the leader
- children have warm, caring relationships with the leader
- children are exposed to the leader's inner dimensions
- children are with the leader in a variety of settings
- children find the leader to be consistent and clear in behaviour and values
- children see the leader's life being consistent with Christian principles
- children are able to have an explanation of the life-style of the leader.

These are challenging thoughts. Children will build their attitudes and values, at least in part, on what they observe and hear from us.

Are there particular guidelines to help? Here are some to think about.

1. Our Christian life is to be natural, not forced. Our lives are to be authentic. We are not putting on a show.

2. We deal with children in a responsible, considerate adult way. We do not have to be 'king of the kids'. Children appreciate adults who treat them as responsible, thinking persons.

3. The variety of experiences is important. It is good for us to be with the children at club, church, sport, community celebrations and picnic days. Thus children see Christian behaviour in different settings.

4. There will be particular 'teachable moments' when the atmosphere is open and children are responsive when we can contribute from our faith. We can say in all sincerity that Jesus is Lord. Such opportunities are to be grasped, and treasured.

5. For an individual child there will be a specific occasion when our presence may be significant. It may be a birthday, or the death of someone close to the child, or it may be a time of celebration. Our presence, interest and words of Christian encouragement will be valuable.

6. The best way by which to teach children respect, reverence and celebration in worship will be through our modelling. We model what we expect, because it is essentially part of our approach. As needed we will exercise leadership to guide and train children in Christian worship.

7. We will need to exercise the gift of discernment — using spiritually alert common sense. From time to time, we will give invitations to the children to come to church, or to Sunday school, or to a church event. But there will be other times when it is clear that a personal invitation, one to one, will be helpful to show our Christian care for a child. Likewise, there will be 'right times' to invite children to trust Jesus as their Saviour and friend. No one can tell when those times are right. The Spirit, and our heart and mind agree, and we respond.

What are the words we will use? They will be simple, sincere and personal. They will be warm. They will affirm the child in his/her discipleship as a 'person who belongs to Jesus'. They will be 'fellow-follower' words, which confirm the support, prayers and personal interest of the leader. The Christian life is made up of many such times of re-commitment of our loyalty to our Lord. Let the child know that you are with him/her on a pilgrimage together.

Task

This is a personal reflection task. Put into a sentence or two your description of what it means to be a Christian. Does it mean 'Jesus is my friend, and he is my guide and strength' or 'Jesus draws me to God' or 'Jesus loves us, each one. He showed this on the cross. I want to serve him'. Can you put the essence of your Christian faith into simple words that at the right time you could share with a child? Write down your words and talk them over with your mentor.

5 FAITH DEVELOPMENT AND PRAYER

Prayer is an activity of the community of faith. The children's club will also use prayer as part of its devotional life. It will, of course, be tuned to the age, attention span and developmental needs of the child members. As children learn about prayer, their faith development will be fostered.

Prayer is mental and verbal fellowship with God. It is spiritual communication. Relationships between God and people give rise to prayer. The essence of prayer is that we are offering our thoughts to God and opening our minds to God in a relationship of sharing.

How is prayer made meaningful to children? Although the minutes spent in prayer at a meeting may be short, there is a key word to deepening the learning, and the experience. The word is participation.

There are aspects of prayer that can be taught and reinforced. For example, the word 'Amen' means 'So let it be'. To say 'Amen' is like a person signing his/her signature at the conclusion of the prayer. The themes of prayer can be explained. Prayers help us say to God, *hooray* (praise), *thanks* (gratitude), *sorry* (confession), *help — for others* (intercession), and *help — for us* (petition).

Participation in prayer will not happen in depth, however, unless the leader adopts methods and strategies that will raise the numbers of children actually involved in preparing and offering prayers in the club.

Here are some ways to increase participation:

- a roster of children to read prayers at club meetings
- children writing prayers at home for use at meetings, and after use then adding them to the club prayer book
- children being asked to offer word or sentence prayers at meetings
- children participating in bidding prayers, with a shared response. Some children can be asked to compose simple litanies
- using antiphonal prayers, by dividing the club into parts, or by children repeating the leader's words
- children taking part in activities which lead to the time of prayer. Here are some suggestions:
  - writing prayers to be attached to balloons
  - poster prayers, with cut-out pictures for illustrations
  - tree of life prayers, with prayers written on cut-out leaves
  - gratitude display prayers; cut-outs, drawings or objects set on a tabletop as symbols of what we are grateful for
- newspaper prayers. Photographs, clippings of stories with short prayers alongside. Intercession is the key
- prayers written as letters to God
- prayer time in small groups, with a leader
- hand-drawn overhead projector transparencies prepared by small groups with drawings and symbols pointing to subjects for prayer
- photographs of children, or of events which can lead into prayer
- creating a worship centre display, to lead into praise
- details from nature. Rocks, shells, autumn leaves, bird feathers, flowers and driftwood pieces could also be used.
- photographic slides, especially of people, to help appreciate others needs.

Remind children from time to time about the nature of prayer. Prayer is being open to God. Children will have some magical ideas about prayer and may see prayer as 'asking for things'. By keeping close to the children both in terms of language and content, you will help them in a process of growth.

Invite children to think about how God answers prayers. Sometimes sharing can occur at worship time when individual children may comment. Make it clear that you would always like children to tell you personally about God's answers to their prayers if they would like to.

There is a gap, of course, between the child's understanding of prayer, and your own. Your task is not suddenly to confront the child with your adult concept, but in empathy to be close to the child, so that you can hear the child's understanding. By listening and responding, you can affirm the child, and perhaps help the young person to enlarge their view and deepen their trust in God.

You will be able to help children too, by once or twice a year issuing them with prayer resources. This may be a card with an appropriate prayer on it. Or it could be a folder with a number of prayers for different occasions. Have some ideas ready for parents if any should ask about prayers for children. Perhaps you can make sure that the church book rack or library has titles on children's prayers available.

All these measures will help children build their concepts of prayer, increase their understanding and use of the language of prayer, and deepen their trust in God in a personal way.

Task

A children's prayer book is an invaluable aid. Use a loose leaf folder. As you find prayers for children from different sources write them into the prayer book. Or type them double-space so that children can read them at club prayer time. As well, as children write and contribute prayers, they can read them aloud at worship, and then they can be placed in the prayer book. Make a start. Point out the first prayer contributed by a club member to your mentor.

6 FAITH DEVELOPMENT AND BIBLE USE

The children's club is not a Sunday school class, nor is it the congregation at worship. It will not be using the Bible in quite the same way as they do. But the club is a Christian community, and it is part of the community of faith, the congregation. That Christian community values the Bible. We are the people of the book, and more deeply, the people of a story.

That story is of God's dealings with people in the Old Testament, and in and through Jesus and the church in the New. The Bible and its story give shape to our faith, belief and character as Christians.

The important factors in the faith development of children, arising from the use of the Bible in a children's club, are that we underline:

● the Bible is valuable to us, as Christians
● the Christian community shapes and is shaped in its life by the Bible
● the Bible gives us our story, from which come our identity and purpose.

Therefore the Bible will be clearly part of club life. A Bible will be seen in the meeting room. Club worship will use the Bible. Activities based on the Bible will often be part of the program. It will be read aloud, and stories from it will be told.

We can turn to some considerations as we think about children and the Bible.

Developmental stages

We remind ourselves that many of the children will not have developed a sense of history as yet. Time spans will not be clear. The difference between the Old Testament and the New Testament in time, or concepts of before Christ

and after Christ, will not be clear for many. But it can be clear that children will learn, perhaps by feeling as much as anything, that the Bible is used because it is valued. It is important. Leaders will model to the children an attitude toward the Bible of significance.

We can expect club children by the nature of their stage of development, to prefer factual information and concrete, literal answers. Leaders need to be aware of that preference. On the one hand 'conceptual' or 'theological' replies to children's questions may be beyond their grasp. But neither will responses that are for us only half-truths be sensible for them in the long term. Sensitive responses that allow children room 'to grow into' and which will not require children to unlearn and relearn will be the most useful. The leader needs to be a thinking Bible-user with a grasp of the child's development. Fortunately experience helps us develop sensitivity.

Engaging the Bible

The most important factor for children's faith development is that children be allowed to explore the Bible text for themselves. When they have opportunities to probe the meaning by questioning and conversing, they will develop their own capacities to grasp meanings, and accept the impact of Bible ideas on their own lives.

When children are free to probe and ask their own questions of the story, they will begin to engage the Bible. In doing so, many of their thinking and feeling skills will be brought to bear. Drama, craft and painting, and other such activities, will help children to engage the Bible.

Questions

Questions will help the process of engaging the Bible. Some questions are 'observation' questions. These can be answered by reading the text and finding information. These will have answers that are right or wrong. Others are 'interpretation' questions that ask children to explore the text and their own experiences to work out answers. 'How did the leper feel when Jesus touched him?' In finding their answer children will work with their own ideas and feelings to make a response. These answers are not right or wrong. They represent the children's own interpretation of the story. The response may be different from yours, but if they have worked it out and it satisfies them we can be pleased at their engagement of the text.

Task

Choose a Bible story such as Luke 19:1–8 (the story of Zaccheus) for personal reading. Imagine that you will be using the story with children and you want them to explore its meanings.

1. Compose two questions that ask children to observe details in the story.

2. Compose three questions that will allow the children to explore the meaning of the story in their terms. The questions should ask them to engage the text, to find out how they feel and think and to discover what changes Jesus' recognition makes to us in our lives. These will be open questions that will lead to children's interpretations. Compose your questions. Share them with your mentor and discuss the outcomes you would expect. Then use the story with children in an activity using your questions. What do you find? Discuss your findings and experiences with your mentor.

Activities

There are appropriate ways for a Club to conduct activities designed to help children engage the Bible. Some suggestions are:

- Play 'finding games' by which children learn to use the index in a Bible or New Testament.
- Include activities by which children learn to use a children's Bible dictionary. An example is Lynn Waller, *International Children's Bible Dictionary* (Fort Worth: Sweet Publishing, 1987).
- Devise games which help children learn the difference between 'gospel' and 'letter' (epistle) in the New Testament.
- Intentionally plan for children to read the Bible aloud at meetings. Avoid calling for volunteers at a moments notice. Give the rostered children some coaching. Ask the Minister for club children to have their turn in reading the Bible at congregational worship.
- Use creative activities by which children have the opportunity 'to work with' a Bible story. Several observation and interpretation questions could prompt their work. Creative activities could include:
  - making a cartoon series of the story by using hand-drawn overhead projector transparencies
- using choral readings of Bible poetry, perhaps in a responsive or antiphonal style, as a part of the club worship
- mime a story, with a child narrating
- write poetry, or free verse, perhaps suggesting an appropriate reading, and several words to begin, for example 'God made . . .'
- painting activity. Use large sheets, brushes at least 2 cm wide, and a range of poster paints and read a story to them several times. Use several questions, with some discussion before beginning painting. Encourage filling the sheets with shapes and colour
- use drama. Here are some passages to consider:

The unjust servant	Matthew 18:23–25
The ten lepers	Luke 17:11–19
Blind Bartimaeus	Luke 18:35–43
	Mark 10:46–52
Zaccheus	Luke 19:1–8
Prodigal son	Luke 15:11–16
Good Samaritan	Luke 10:29–37
David and Goliath	1 Samuel 17

- make tape plays. Having the use of a large recorder with a free-standing microphone will help. Suitable stories are:

Jesus walks on water	Matthew 14:22–34
The large catch of fish	Luke 5:1–12
Man through the roof	Mark 2:1–12
Call of Samuel	1 Samuel 1 and 3
Elisha heals a boy	2 Kings 4:8–37
Naaman the leper	2 Kings 5:1–19
Shadrach, and all	Daniel 3
Daniel in the lions' den	Daniel 6

- use cards with simple line drawings of people who met Jesus, ask children to recall the episodes, and to search those people's thoughts and feelings. Some interpretation questions will help the process
- poster or banner activity. Prepare designs that depict a key thought from a Bible story. Any story with Jesus at the centre could be used
- clay or plasticene modelling and making of Bible scenes. Story scenes can be made, giving children creative work with their hands. Model the key moment in the story.

Many of these activities are suitable for small group work. That increases the opportunity for conversation with a leader and amongst the children. Faith sharing can occur in that context.

Resources for home use

Many churches have contact persons who will arrange for subscriptions to Bible study guides and devotional notes for members of the congregation. There are materials suitable for children. Encourage children to participate. Conversation with parents may assist.

As well, from time to time, arrange to give all children in the club a worksheet that asks them to find, read and explore a Bible story. A method for reporting back can be included on the sheet, and that will give you the opportunity to listen to and talk with children about their discoveries.

The key

The key to faith development through Bible use lies in children bringing their own logic to the Bible story, having to observe its contents, and then in their own terms interpreting its meaning themselves. Children's faith development will occur when 'they work with the word'. It follows, of course, that adults need to be willing to give freedom to children to explore and give their ideas (which may differ from an adult view).

As you are able to model that same willingness to engage the Bible, and share your own understandings in empathy with children, you will be contributing to their growth.

Task

Take a Bible passage (for example Mark 1:16–20, the calling of the first disciples) for your personal study. Then work out a way to have club members 'work with' that story. Develop an activity, perhaps using one of the suggestions mentioned above, so that children have to observe the facts of the story, and also interpret its meaning to a person in the story, and also for themselves. You may like to plan the activity with your assistants, and then use it in a meeting. Show your written plans and later describe your results to your mentor.

7 ENFOLDING THE CHILDREN IN THE CONGREGATION

Children's faith can be fostered as they are enfolded in the fellowship of a congregation. Why is this important? The worshipping congregation is the core of the faith community. That is where people are equipped as Christians. It is the special fellowship. The children's club needs to have many linkages with the congregation, with the involvement of the club leaders being uppermost.

There are several parts to this task. One is to affirm children who are in worship with their parents. Another is to help children come to worship who are not otherwise linked. Another is to help the congregation itself recognise the children's presence and to increase their involvement. Many people in the congregation need to be joining you in showing that each child matters.

More ideas about this important area are included in Chapter 8 'Outreach — the children's club reaching out'.

8 WORSHIP IN THE CHILDREN'S CLUB

If you have worked through this learning program on faith development, and also the storytelling segment of the learning program 'Conducting Children's Club Programs' you will have become clearer about the purposes and content which are related to worship in the club. The concluding tasks in this learning program relate to planning worship in the club.

There are several guidelines for you to consider:

1. Use a theme for the worship time. This means that the several elements of the worship time will fit together. There is a linkage between parts.

2. Choose a theme that arises out of the 'real world of the child'. This is where an adult must work to discover what is the real world for children. What are the subjects that claim their attention, arouse their curiosity, or relate to their fears? Who are their current heroes? Observation of children and listening to their conversations are necessary to gain entry to the real world of the child. Find the theme from your insights into 'their world'. Then that theme can serve to link God's Word with their world.

3. In writing the planning notes for your worship outline, use action statements that help you visualise what you and the children will be doing. For example, rather than writing 'Opening' or 'Call to worship', use a sentence such as 'The leader calls us to worship, explains our purpose, and introduces the theme "Hands to serve God" '. Or instead of 'Prayers for others', write 'Prayers will be said by two children, after other children have commented on their "For others" posters'.

4. Maximise the involvement of children by finding ways to increase participation. Responsive prayers can be used simply by asking children to remember a response, and giving them cue words. An overhead projector is valuable for litanies, as well as songs. Remember, also, the value of actions and movement in songs to increase participation and use of the senses.

5. Value the seasons of the church year, for these arise from the key events in the life and work of Jesus. By raising themes that link the key events and children's real world, you will increase their recognition of Jesus as the centre of faith. We are people of the Jesus story. We cannot explain ourselves unless we draw on the story of Jesus.

Task

Write out your plans for several worship segments. Choose the respective themes, write out the action directions, and plan for maximum participation.
Plan for worship times of differing lengths:
1. **to contain a Bible reading and prayer**
2. **to contain a song, Bible reading and prayer**
3. **to contain a song, Bible reading, a story, and prayers which arise from an activity in the program.**
You may have prepared similar to these already. Prepare new plans for use in the future. Try to include values from this learning program on faith development.
Show your plans to your mentor. If you have already used any of them in the club, describe your learnings from the experience.

9 DRAWING IT TOGETHER

This chapter has given an overview of the factors that foster faith development in children. There are other factors, of course, such as home influence, school, peers, and other recreational settings in which the child is placed. We know however, that our part in the child's faith development will be vital. We want our part to be positive.

What we are and do counts for much. We are the sermon for children.

SELF-ASSESSMENT

When you have completed the tasks outlined in this program, then you will be ready for this assessment activity with the aid of your mentor.

It is a joint activity, with conversation, through which your mentor will endorse the completion of the tasks. The mentor will be looking at your faith development practices in the club, and helping you assess whether you have performed the various functions according to the suggested standards.

Levels of performance: Place an 'X' in the appropriate box. If, because of special circumstances, a component was not applicable, or impossible to execute, an 'X' may be placed in the 'not applicable' box. All items should receive a n/a, good or excellent response. If any item receives a none, poor or fair response, then you and the mentor will need to determine what additional activities are required in order to complete that component. It may mean having more practice, and then inviting your mentor to observe you and the club in action again. The aim is a personal one — to be able to foster children's growth in the Christian faith with assurance and empathy.

Rating scale for all items: N/A | None | Poor | Fair | Good | Excellent

1   As leader, I visit each child or family at home at least once ☐ ☐ ☐ ☐ ☐ ☐

or

I organise, and delegate visiting of each child and family at least once. ☐ ☐ ☐ ☐ ☐ ☐

2   As leader, I treat children with respect by . . .
a.   calling children by name ☐ ☐ ☐ ☐ ☐ ☐

b.   praising and affirming children ☐ ☐ ☐ ☐ ☐ ☐

c.   speaking personally with each child ☐ ☐ ☐ ☐ ☐ ☐

d.   being fair to each child. ☐ ☐ ☐ ☐ ☐ ☐

3   As leader, I reprimand children, if required,
a.   away from the group ☐ ☐ ☐ ☐ ☐ ☐

b.   by asking them to describe their behaviour ☐ ☐ ☐ ☐ ☐ ☐

c.   asking them to describe their new behaviour. ☐ ☐ ☐ ☐ ☐ ☐

4   As leader, I anticipate difficulties or behaviour problems beforehand, and ensure that
a.   adequate supervision is available for particular children ☐ ☐ ☐ ☐ ☐ ☐

b.   rules are obeyed ☐ ☐ ☐ ☐ ☐ ☐

c.   misbehaviour is treated firmly, fairly and promptly. ☐ ☐ ☐ ☐ ☐ ☐

5   As leader, I witness to my Christian faith by
a.   regular worship attendance ☐ ☐ ☐ ☐ ☐ ☐

b.   pursuing personal devotional life ☐ ☐ ☐ ☐ ☐ ☐

c.   modelling attitudes of care and fairness ☐ ☐ ☐ ☐ ☐ ☐

d.   sharing my faith in conversation. ☐ ☐ ☐ ☐ ☐ ☐

6   As leader, I model attitudes to worship which show reverence, respect, joy, enthusiasm and celebration. ☐ ☐ ☐ ☐ ☐ ☐

7   As leader, I invite children to . . .
a.   participate in the congregation ☐ ☐ ☐ ☐ ☐ ☐

b.   attend Sunday school ☐ ☐ ☐ ☐ ☐ ☐

c.   join in church family activities. ☐ ☐ ☐ ☐ ☐ ☐

8   As leader, I encourage individual children in their spiritual growth by
a.   speaking personally with individual children ☐ ☐ ☐ ☐ ☐ ☐

b.   inviting children, as appropriate, to be Jesus' followers. ☐ ☐ ☐ ☐ ☐ ☐

9   As leader, I use 'small groups' for children to participate in
a.   activities to engage the Christian faith ☐ ☐ ☐ ☐ ☐ ☐

b.   sharing conversation ☐ ☐ ☐ ☐ ☐ ☐

c.   Bible story activity ☐ ☐ ☐ ☐ ☐ ☐

	N/A	None	Poor	Fair	Good	Excellent

d. shared prayer activity. ☐☐☐☐☐☐

10 As leader, I utilise 'key events' of the church calendar to introduce elements of the Christ story to children. ☐☐☐☐☐☐

11 As leader, I teach children to pray by coaching them to write prayers and use them at club meetings. ☐☐☐☐☐☐

12 As leader, I provide children's resources for children to . . .
a. pray at home ☐☐☐☐☐☐

b. read the Bible at home. ☐☐☐☐☐☐

13 As leader, I encourage children to acknowledge answers to prayer by . . .
a. talking to me personally ☐☐☐☐☐☐

b. seeking comments, on occasions, at meetings. ☐☐☐☐☐☐

14 As leader, I give children opportunity to read the Bible aloud at meetings, regularly. ☐☐☐☐☐☐

15 As leader, I teach the members to
a. say Grace at meals ☐☐☐☐☐☐

b. use a variety of Graces over time. ☐☐☐☐☐☐

16 As leader, I ask the leaders, at planning meetings, to pray for the church, the congregation, the club, the children, and for each other. ☐☐☐☐☐☐

Mentor's endorsement

I declare that (leader's name) ....
has completed the self-assessment tasks of this learning program with good or excellent markings.

Signed............................... (mentor)............(date)

Chapter 8

Outreach — the children's club reaching out

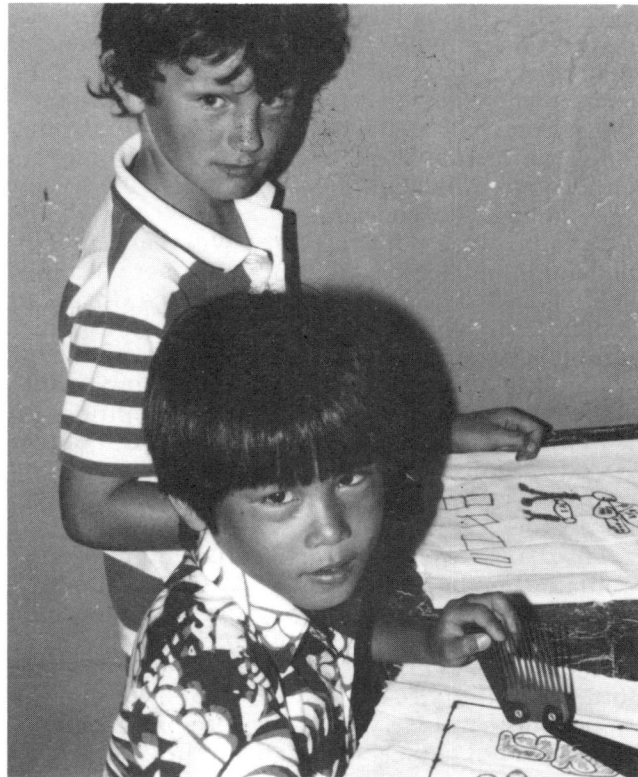

There are several dimensions to 'outreach'. The children's club will be one of the instruments to help the congregation in its outreach work. On the other hand, the club is an instrument to help its members 'reach-out' to the wider church and its work, and to the neighbourhood.

Definitions

These are the definitions of 'outreach' and 'reaching-out' that are used in this learning program.

Outreach: those endeavours of the church to enlist people and make disciples, equipping them to be responsible and contributing members of the church.

Reaching-out: those endeavours of the church to expand church people's consciousness of the world-wide fellowship of the church, and the church's service to a needy world from neighbourhood to globe in scope.

This learning program deals with a number of the tasks that promote outreach and reaching-out. A club will benefit from the implementation of action plans that have been discussed by the leaders. Such action plans will embrace segments from other chapters in this book, especially 'Conducting children's club programs' (Chapter 4) and 'Pastoral care and faith development' (Chapter 7).

1 REASONS FOR OUTREACH

There are several reasons why a club needs to be concerned about outreach.

First, outreach is an element of healthy and effective club management. Club life will be more vibrant, and more diverse programs are possible if you have lots of children and adults to support them. Of course, some situations are such that a club may include all the eligible children in the locality. This can occur in rural towns. But in many places there are children who could belong but who may not know of the opportunity to be in a club. Club leaders should not remain satisfied with a handful of children. The club will come alive when there are new children joining. This element alone will give a growing edge to your club.

Second, outreach to children will result in providing many with their first contact with the gospel, and their first involvement in a Christian group. Many will come, also, from church-related families. In either case, contact with Christian leadership and exposure to Christian habits and ways is important for children's development in the Christian faith. Children will grow out of the need to belong to a children's club, but we remember, they will never grow out of the need for Jesus.

Third, outreach needs to be an element of the club method because the club is an instrument of the congregation with two purposes. One purpose is to be a seedbed for the faith development of children. The second is to be a form of ministry to children and their families as a part of the ministry of the congregation. The club does not exist separate from the congregation, but as an important aspect of its ministry. On many occasions, the presence of a new child at club meetings will be the first involvement of a family with the church. The club can alert the congregation to the presence of a new family, just as the congregation may point out new families to the children's club and have their children involved.

2 THE DANGER OF ISOLATION

A children's club needs active linkages with the congregation. The congregation needs to be feeding leaders to the club, and accepting the club as a vital part of its ministry to families and the faith development of children. Obversely, leaders who prefer to work in isolation from the congregation will loosen linkages with the community of faith. Such leadership can be destructive rather than constructive in the total ministry of the local church.

It is true that some in the congregation and its leadership will not have grasped the significance of the children's club as an aspect of the ministry of the congregation. Sometimes the club leader has to 'blow the trumpet' to remind the congregation. If a leader reaches the point where he or she feels neglected and alone in the work,

then new linkages need to be forged. Either the congregation and its leadership have lost the vision of its ministry through the club, or the club leaders have lost the vision of the community of faith in whose ministry the club is an integral part.

Linkages are important. The club has an action plan for outreach, because it is to act in concert with the congregation.

3 DISCOVERING NEW CHILDREN

New children will be discovered if two things are happening. First, you are running an effective and exciting program that holds and interests children, and is valued by parents. Second, your members are encouraged to bring friends to the club. Much of your recruitment will result from these two aspects. Children respond to lively programs and personable leadership. It is difficult to conserve or enlarge numbers if you are not providing positive programs. Particular sources of new children are:

1. Transfers of church membership as a family moves into your neighbourhood. The Minister or the secretary of the Elders Council will tell you of these. Movement to a new locality can be worrisome for children, as probably they have left friends behind. They, as much as their parents, need to be made welcome.

2. Families visiting the congregation for worship. They may be new to the area, or are, perhaps, 'shopping round' for a church family. You can play an immediate role in introducing yourself and welcoming the children. Many young families look for a church that will make their children feel at home.

The discovery of new children may be assisted by information posters placed in key places. Suitable venues are community health centres, kindergarten and primary school notice boards, children's library and shopping centre notice boards. Such information posters need to be directed to parents. Show the age group you cater for, the name of the church, address of meeting place, normal meeting times, and two telephone numbers.

Here are four strategies designed to discover new children.

1. Provide, occasionally, programs that are specifically 'Bring a Friend' nights. Advertise

76

this well by informing parents perhaps a month beforehand, and enlist their encouragement for their children to invite their friends to attend. Church notice sheet publicity will also assist. Provide a program that emphasises involvement. The program does not have to be unusual or gimmicky, but it should be well run, giving visitors an idea of what happens normally in the club.

2. Use ongoing reminders to children that they can invite new children to join. Children from school, or children new to their street can be invited.

3. Incentive programs. Occasionally an incentive aspect can be built into the club 'points' competition. If you are running a team competition over a series of meetings, points can be given to a team that brings a new member and who comes for at least three meetings.

4. Setting targets. In the process of building the membership of the club, you can set targets with achievable numbers. For example, if you have fifteen members, you can set a target for twenty regular attending members. A 'thermometer' chart can help children see progress toward the target. The approach will enlist their involvement. A special picnic outing, or a 'dress-up' program can be scheduled to celebrate when the target is accomplished.

Task

What is the size of your club? What target could you set that is reasonable and achievable, and could be accomplished over the next four months, to increase the number of children involved? What strategies would you employ? When you are ready, share your ideas with your mentor.

4 WELCOMING AND ASSIMILATING

As soon as a family comes to your attention because a new child comes to children's club, then the Minister and the elders need to be informed. The welcoming and assimilating of new families to the ambit of the congregation is a wider responsibility, and the club leaders need to be assured that others from the congregation are involved also. Nevertheless, the club

leadership will play an important part as partners in the process.

In order to welcome and help new children to be assimilated into the club, several steps can be taken. These can be listed in this way.

● Learn the child's name as quickly as possible, and use the name frequently.

● Ensure that the child meets other children and is placed in a small group immediately. Make sure that the child meets the other leaders too.

● Arrange to visit the child's home so that you can have an enrolment discussion with the parents.

● Make contact with the child again, especially to ensure that he/she is becoming part of the club fellowship. Give information that the other children may know, but may not have been given to a new member. For example, others may know about the parent's night, or a weekend camp that lie in the near future, but could catch the new family unawares.

Task

Check the learning program on 'Administration' to find out about enrolment procedures. If you have not done so, decide on your enrolment policy. Consider how important these can be for welcoming and assimilating a new child. Describe to your mentor the procedures you will follow.

5 CONSERVING MEMBERSHIP

Children respond to personal attention. A leader should aim to speak personally to as many of the children as possible at meetings. A personal exchange counts for much, and will help you conserve membership.

You and your assistants will find it useful to develop a system of follow-up for absentee children. The person who is absent and is not missed may fall into believing that it does not matter if he/she is present or not. A policy similar to this could be followed.

1. Mark the attendance roll at each meeting. This can be done unobtrusively (there is no need to call the roll), but this will immediately remind you of the children not present.

2. Other children may know the reasons for a child's absence — not at school today; home sick; away on holidays. Whether there is information or not, one leader may volunteer

to telephone the family to inquire, perhaps the next day.

3. If a child has been absent for two or more meetings because of sickness, then a card can be sent, with a personal message. Special club cards can be simply made.

4. If a child is absent without discovery of a reason for two meetings or more, then a friendship visit can be made.

It is helpful if parents are aware that you will miss their child's presence, and that it will help you if you have received an apology especially if the child is unwell.

An attendance wall chart can also be helpful especially if over a short term a team competition is being used and attendance is noted as one factor. An apology because of unavoidable absence (sickness, holidays, family commitments) can still count as attendance.

The practice of greeting parents before or after meetings, so underlining the interest of the leaders in their children, is commended. Leaders can take turns in this important task.

Task

Design a simple hand-lettered club card that could be sent to sick children. Show this to your mentor, and outline the action plan you and your assistants are following for keeping contact with absentee children.

6 LINKAGES TO THE CONGREGATION

Part of the function of the children's club is to be an instrument for children's faith development, and as well to be a means for children and their families to become part of the congregation. The children's club is an aspect of the ministry of the congregation. The club is an outreach arm of the congregation at work.

Ideally, both the congregation and the club have a concern to see children being embraced by the congregation. The club leader may have to facilitate this by speaking out for children and seeking opportunities for children to be involved and to serve in the congregation. By pressing for these, the club, the children and the congregation will benefit.

Here are some strategies.

● Ask for children to be included on the Bible

reading roster for worship and provide them with some coaching.

● Ask for children of the club to have opportunities to participate in worship with a special song, or sacred dance, or mimed story, or a drama.

● Arrange if you can, on occasions, for some children to be included on the worship planning committee.

● Ask for information about the club to be given through church notice sheets, or church announcements.

● Arrange for displays of club activities to be placed for viewing by the congregation. Posters, banners, charts and photographs will be of interest to adults in the congregation.

● Encourage arrangements so that children can adopt a grandparent. Some older people will enjoy such an arrangement, whereby they can develop an interest in the club member. Perhaps they will sit together at worship. Such a scheme can be developed informally, but it may well begin by the club having a special program to which older members of the congregation are specifically invited.

● There will be some children who will come to worship alone. As soon as this is noted, the club leaders may be able to suggest a church family (who may not have children of the same age) with whom the child could identify. They sit together.

● The club leaders will be advocates for the children to be involved in the congregation at worship. Sometimes obvious details are overlooked, such as not giving children hymnbooks or service sheets the same as adults are. Likewise if the practice is to have name-bars or buttons for the adults of the congregation, similar patterns need to follow for the children. The club leaders may become conscious of these matters before others in the congregation. To speak up will facilitate the outreach of the congregation to children and their families.

● Some segments of club programs can be used to prepare children for participation in worship. For example, learning the Lord's Prayer, or the words of the Gloria, or some of the responses ('The Lord be with you: and also with you') can be learned in club meetings.

Establishing linkages between children and the congregation will not happen overnight. But it is important for the outreach work of the club that children come to know the congregation and feel part of the faith community.

Task

You know your situation. Use the ideas of this segment on 'linkages' to prompt positive ideas for forging links between children of the club and the congregation in your situation. What have you and your assistants planned as your next step? Discuss your plans with your mentor. What date have you chosen to take the next step?

7 AN OPEN CLUB

An open club displays an attitude of welcome and acceptance. Such a club is always keen to have parents call to watch, or the minister to come as often as possible, or children to bring friends even for one night. With that attitude the concern for outreach is well in hand.

Occasionally, however, the club needs to offer a program that is well advertised and sets out to invite interested people to come. Such occasional open nights allow congregational members committed to the outreach work of the club to visit and support the work.

Who are the key people to invite to a club open night?

- children who are members, and their friends
- parents, and other children of the family
- other relatives of the children, particularly grandparents
- ministers and elders
- youth group leaders (for they will want to be known especially to the older children of the club)
- 'adoptive' grandparents
- interested adults.

The program format could take one of several forms. The content could be:

- a normal program with the visitors mainly observing
- a program with a range of activities designed for participation by old and young together
- a program in which a major part is entertainment by the children.

Whatever choice is made, some key segments should be aimed towards all age involvement and conversation. Keep the program well to time, no longer than usual so that it is punchy and quick moving. Coach children so that they can act as hosts and servers of supper. Advertise the program well. Give specific invitations to particular people you would like to attend.

As club leader, plan in detail with your assistants. On the open night, however, keep yourself as free as possible to oversee the program and to be available to visitors. Open programs will take time and effort to plan and conduct, but they will be a sign of vibrancy and openness to the congregation and the neighbourhood. They show a willingness to reach out.

Task

How would you conduct an open night with your club? What type of program would work best? Parents, of course, like to see their children accomplishing and participating. They enjoy seeing their child make social progress. Make a list of four program segments that would be appropriate for an open night program. Discuss your written ideas with your mentor.

8 INTRODUCING CHILDREN TO THE WIDER CHURCH

It is a valuable lesson for children and adults alike to discover that the church is bigger than our congregation. We all benefit from large gatherings that help us recognise the wider church. Christians need the sense of community that comes from our home group experiences and the fellowship of a congregation. But every now and then we gain from being in the larger gathering.

Children will learn from exposure to the wider church. Explanations about the church begin to make sense through experience. How can this be done for children? There are several types of activities that will be valuable.

- Combined programs with neighbouring clubs, where two, three or four clubs meet for an evening in a large facility. Because of the larger numbers, a key visitor can be the centre point. A clown, mime artist or a chalk artist could be a possibility.
- Rallies for children are sometimes arranged by Presbyteries or Synods. These are sometimes of the outdoor picnic type, with appropriate outdoor activities. Combined worship may conclude the program. These can be excellent when they are designed around family participation.
- Holding a children's camp with another club is another way of letting children experience

something of the wider church. Country/city links are helpful in this regard. An alternative is a country/city visit with children billeted with families, or even using a church hall for accommodation.

- Some Synods conduct programs such as Kids' Campout. Large numbers of children from many churches participate in such events. Child-centred programming is a feature. Children's concepts of the church, and their place in the church are effectively expanded by the experience.

- Parishes with several congregations will have, perhaps annually, assemblies for worship and celebration for the whole parish. These occasions are also valuable for children. It is specially helpful if segments of the service have been specifically planned with the needs of children in mind. Movement, colour, means for participation, and contemporary music are helpful to children.

- *Special note*: such strategies as these will require signed parental permission forms, unless the families are attending together. If you have not done so, check through the learning program 'Administration' on the need for parental permission and consent forms for activities other than regular meetings.

These are aspects of reaching-out to understand the breadth of the wider church. These opportunities will expand the children's minds and experiences of the church.

Task

What opportunities are available for you to let children experience the wider church? List some possibilities. Choose one that seems most worthwhile to you. List three action steps you would need to take to begin planning such an event. Discuss your action steps, and concept, with your mentor.

9 REACHING-OUT IN SERVICE AND PROJECT WORK

The fundamentals of service and project work, which are well developed in many adult areas of the church's life, can be established in the children's club. The purpose will be to make a difference in some way to the wider work of the church or to some situation of need in the neighbourhood, or beyond. But the gains made

by children are significant. Leaders concerned for the emotional and spiritual development of their members will recognise the educational and formative value of these experiences for children.

What are some of the benefits in being involved in reaching-out service projects? What will they do for Club members? They will:

- help the development of their empathy, sympathy and compassion. The children will be broadened. They will learn a little of the scope of Christian love.
- help their planning, organising and decision-making skills. Children need to be active in this process. As much as possible children need to discuss issues and make decisions.
- help them learn that people can make a difference for others, if they are prepared to take action.
- help them shape their skills as moral and spiritual agents.

Wise leaders recognising the educational impact of such projects will realise that the learning value for children lies in them being the 'doers' rather than being moved around by adults. The skills of the adults will be needed as facilitators, coaches and supporters. Children need to have their 'hands-on' as much of the action as possible for them to gain the potential value of the project.

The church can be grateful when:

- children are becoming sensitive to people's needs
- children are learning about the church's work in a needy world
- children are opening their eyes to the neighbourhood, or even further afield
- foundations are being established in the consciousness of children and young people for possible future or long term ministries.

Whatever the nature of the project or service, you and your assistants need to value the training opportunities for the children of the club, as well as a way of contributing to an area of need.

Types of projects

Broadly service projects can be developed along these lines:

1. helping people, with direct contact

2. undertaking a task which will benefit a situation perhaps removed by distance

3. raising money to alleviate a human need.

Projects of the direct helping type include giving a concert in a children's ward, visiting an elderly persons' home to provide visitors or entertainment, in small groups calling on elderly people in their homes, delivering greetings from the church to particular homes, or knitting rug squares for a particular person. In these projects children will meet people, and there will be some exchange of warmth.

Projects that will benefit people removed from the children involve collecting used stamps for missions; collecting used spectacles for mission projects; organising a pencil drive to send pencils to mission schools; collecting toys for a distant situation. In these cases, there is need for information beforehand, and letters of acknowledgment after to give children a sense of accomplishment.

Money raising projects by children can be intended for such purposes as those mentioned in Care and Share in Lent, or the Christmas Bowl appeal, or World Vision child sponsorship. Children can conduct such money raising efforts as setting up and running a small fete (providing there are some willing adults to coach, facilitate and oversee progress, as well as parents who will support the endeavour); organising an evening on the theme of a '5 cent night' when children run activities and games where participation costs 5 cents for anything. The activities are chosen to be run by children for children and their parents. The importance of these approaches is that children can do much of the organising and conducting of the program. That is both fun and a training experience.

In all these, information for the children is vital. They need to be hearing about the people, the agencies, the places and the needs to be met. Gaining information suitable and diverse enough for decision-making by children is important.

How do you involve children in contributing ideas? Here is a good opportunity to let children learn about and participate in 'brainstorming'. This works on the basis of people's ideas stimulating further ideas, and not stopping to comment. Here are the rules:

- the leader explains the rules
- begin with a broad statement of the issue to be decided
- call for suggestions
- every suggestion is accepted
- every suggestion is written on a board or chart
- no comments or assessments of the suggestions are made yet. There are no speeches

- continue in quick fire style until no further suggestions are made
- then proceed back over the list seeking comments about any of the suggestions. Unpopular suggestions can be crossed through, until the popular choices show.

This method could be used both for deciding on what to do as a project, and how to do a project.

Sometimes, however, some community need will come to your attention as club leader. You consider that it would be one that the club could handle to their benefit. Rather than announce that this will be done, take time to sound out the older children and gain their interest. Let them make decisions. Ask them how they think the rest of the club could be involved. Let them talk with others, and follow their advice about how to enlist the club. As much decision making as possible needs to be with children.

Stickability

It is in the area of supporting children to see things through that the leaders will need to give energy. Children will tire quickly, and will not realise how much work is required in undertaking a project. Leaders wil need to keep the goals to a sensible size as well as providing the back-up and the warming-up of supporters.

How often should a club undertake such a project? Perhaps once a year for some reaching-out project. Every second year the project could be more demanding.

Such service work needs to be adventurous for children. It needs to allow them to find enjoyment in helping. There will be many gains for them and their development with warm guidance from their leaders. Because of the immaturity of children, they will need careful direction and support as well as encouraging relationships.

Program segments and key visitors

Widening children's horizons will be helped significantly by activities in club programs with reaching-out themes. For example, playing the World Card game (from UNICEF) introduces children to some of the terms and concepts related to third world societies and our own. Slides sets of mission activity, or video or audio tapes from missionaries, or particularly the visiting speaker who can let children hear of some field where the church is reaching out in its work, will be significant in children's expanding view of the church at work. The learning program on 'Conducting Club Programs' gives further guidance about the wise use of visiting speakers.

There are particular Scriptures which can be used as your foundation, both in your private study and as a basis for worship in the club. These include:

Jesus' two great commandments	Luke 10:25–28
You did it for me — Jesus' story	Matthew 25:31–46
The parable of the good Samaritan	Luke 10:25–37
A cup of cold water	Matthew 10:42
Go into all the world	Matthew 28:19–20
The Spririt of the Lord is upon me	Luke 4:17–20

9 DRAWING IT TOGETHER

This learning program has outlined ways for a club to make two thrusts: 'outreach' to draw in new children and to act in concert with and on behalf of the congregation as an arm of its ministry; and in 'reaching-out' to expand children's concepts of the wider church and its work and service to people. The fruits of these endeavours will be long lasting in these children. Their faith development will be enhanced. Skills will be established. They will begin to sense the concern that Christians have for each other and the needy. They will have made first steps in building their understanding of the church as both local and universal.

The children will need many more experiences of these types as they grow. If we can help children learn that people who care and work together can make a difference for others, we have laid a good foundation for their future as contributing Christians.

SELF ASSESSMENT

When you have completed the tasks outlined in this program, then you will be ready for this assessment activity with the aid of your mentor.

It is a joint activity, with conversation, through which your mentor will endorse the completion of the tasks. The mentor will be looking at the 'outreach' and 'reaching-out' practices in the club and helping you assess whether you have performed the various functions according to the suggested standards.

Levels of performance: Place an 'X' in the appropriate box. If, because of special circumstances, a component was not applicable, or impossible to execute, an 'X' may be placed in the 'not applicable' box. All items should receive a n/a, good or excellent response. If any item receives a none, poor or fair response, then you and the mentor will need to determine what additional activities are required in order to complete that component. It may mean improving a policy, or sharpening a procedure, and then inviting your mentor to observe and discuss further the measures you are taking. The aim is for the club to be active in 'outreach' as an instrument of the congregation, and as well through 'reaching-out' to expand the children's horizons of the caring church.

		N/A	None	Poor	Fair	Good	Excellent
1	As leader, my assistants and I follow an action plan for club outreach, which includes:						
a.	methods for increasing membership	☐	☐	☐	☐	☐	☐
b.	methods for conserving membership.	☐	☐	☐	☐	☐	☐
2	As leader, I visit each child or family as required to aid their assimilation	☐	☐	☐	☐	☐	☐
	or						
	I organise and delegate visiting of each child and family at home as required to aid their assimilation.	☐	☐	☐	☐	☐	☐
3	As leader, I enlist the Minister, elders, in visiting of children and families by						
a.	informing them of new families	☐	☐	☐	☐	☐	☐
b.	indicating special or crisis needs.	☐	☐	☐	☐	☐	☐

4 As leader, I employ an absentee follow-up system that includes:

	N/A	None	Poor	Fair	Good	Excellent
a. marking of attendance roll	☐	☐	☐	☐	☐	☐
b. telephone enquiry concerning a child's absence from a meeting	☐	☐	☐	☐	☐	☐
c. sending of appropriate card for sickness, holidays, etc.	☐	☐	☐	☐	☐	☐
d. visiting of child (by self or assistant) if absent for two meetings.	☐	☐	☐	☐	☐	☐

5 As leader, I promote and publicise the club by:

	N/A	None	Poor	Fair	Good	Excellent
a. information posters in schools and public places	☐	☐	☐	☐	☐	☐
b. information in congregation's notice bulletins	☐	☐	☐	☐	☐	☐
c. information in church directory.	☐	☐	☐	☐	☐	☐

6 As leader, I conduct incentive programs to encourage:

	N/A	None	Poor	Fair	Good	Excellent
a. members to be present at each meeting	☐	☐	☐	☐	☐	☐
b. members to report sickness and record apology	☐	☐	☐	☐	☐	☐
c. members to bring new members.	☐	☐	☐	☐	☐	☐

7 As leader, I welcome newcomers by:

	N/A	None	Poor	Fair	Good	Excellent
a. meeting parents at enrolment interview	☐	☐	☐	☐	☐	☐
b. welcoming and introducing child to other club members and assistants	☐	☐	☐	☐	☐	☐
c. greeting parents before/ after meetings.	☐	☐	☐	☐	☐	☐

8 As leader, I invite children to:

	N/A	None	Poor	Fair	Good	Excellent
a. participate in the congregation	☐	☐	☐	☐	☐	☐
b. attend Sunday school	☐	☐	☐	☐	☐	☐
c. join in church family activities.	☐	☐	☐	☐	☐	☐

9 As leader, I negotiate for:

	N/A	None	Poor	Fair	Good	Excellent
a. club members to read lessons on occasions	☐	☐	☐	☐	☐	☐
b. club members to provide song/dance/mime, etc. for worship on occasions	☐	☐	☐	☐	☐	☐
c. club information to be presented to the congregation	☐	☐	☐	☐	☐	☐
d. club posters, work, photographs to be displayed for the congregation.	☐	☐	☐	☐	☐	☐

10 As leader, I negotiate for children to be incorporated in the congregation by using such methods as:

	N/A	None	Poor	Fair	Good	Excellent
a. children adopting a grandparent	☐	☐	☐	☐	☐	☐
b. lone children adopting a church family	☐	☐	☐	☐	☐	☐

The rating columns for both columns are: N/A, None, Poor, Fair, Good, Excellent

c. ensuring children have name bars or buttons according to congregation's practice for adults. ☐☐☐☐☐☐

11 As leader, I arrange for occasional club programs to involve:
a. parents and their children ☐☐☐☐☐☐

b. Ministers and elders ☐☐☐☐☐☐

c. youth group leaders ☐☐☐☐☐☐

d. 'adoptive' grandparents and families. ☐☐☐☐☐☐

12 As leader, I arrange for the club to participate in:
a. children's rallies and picnic days ☐☐☐☐☐☐

b. joint club activities ☐☐☐☐☐☐

c. overnight activities (campouts, sleep-ins, etc.) with other clubs. ☐☐☐☐☐☐

13 As leader, I utilise program segments to give understanding and involvement in the church's reaching-out work, such as:
a. social welfare programs ☐☐☐☐☐☐

b. 'missions' at home ☐☐☐☐☐☐

c. 'missions' overseas. ☐☐☐☐☐☐

14 As leader, I facilitate the program to support children and/or the club to participate in programs such as:
a. World Vision 'foodbusters' ☐☐☐☐☐☐

b. sponsor a child ☐☐☐☐☐☐

c. contact with and support of missionaries. ☐☐☐☐☐☐

d. or similar programs developed in our region. ☐☐☐☐☐☐

15 As leader, I work with the club to undertake a project locally for the church or neighbourhood with features such as:
a. as much decision making by children as possible ☐☐☐☐☐☐

b. a design to increase children's knowledge of community work. ☐☐☐☐☐☐

Mentor's endorsement

I declare that (leader's name) ....
has completed the self-assessment tasks of this learning program with good or excellent markings.

Signed.................................. (mentor).........(date)

Chapter 9

Leadership and team building in a children's club

This learning program turns our attention away from children for a time in order to concentrate on the club's leadership team. How can the club leader work with assistants, conveners, resource people and others from the congregation and build team-spirit amongst them? This team will range from teenagers to adults with their own children, from the immature to the mature, and persons with low levels to high levels of competence and confidence. Building a team will enhance the usefulness of the club to its members, and make the work enjoyable to its leadership team. Leadership and team-building do not occur through one single factor. There are several dimensions.

1 TAKING A TEAM APPROACH

It is better to have a team conducting a club for these reasons:

- a team spreads the work load, and also the opportunities
- a team increases the potential for growth, in all respects
- a team provides children with a diverse range of models and friends. Individual children will relate more closely to some than to others on the team. Male and female should be on the team
- a team allows for a variety of skill levels to be available
- a team provides a seedbed for the development of young people as leaders
- a team provides for better supervision and safety for children
- A team can prevent negligent behaviour by an adult, as team members accept responsibility for each other

- a team approach provides a training ground for a successor to the club leader.

The one-person-band in charge of a club is rarely healthy for the club, the children or the congregation. Strenuous efforts should be given to team-building. The club leader will need both to lead and draw people together as a team. We begin to examine some of the factors which are involved.

2 ASPECTS OF LEADERSHIP

Leadership is exercised through influencing the efforts of an individual or a group towards fulfilment of a goal or task. The results of leadership may be the accomplishment of some objective by a group. The process of leading may require a variety of styles and approaches.

For example, authoritarian leaders may use a style of force and compulsion. That is rarely appropriate in a children's club although it could be necessary if the building caught fire, and you had the safety of many as your responsibility. What leadership processes or styles are appropriate for a Christian club leader?

It is helpful to think about some episodes in Jesus' ministry. They give us glimpses of the leadership styles he used, and which we can value.

- 'Follow me . . .' (Mark 1:17)

He enlisted people by invitation; they left their situations voluntarily.

- 'I am the good shepherd.' (John 10:11)

He offered a pastor's care, leading people safely to places of refreshment.

- 'Sit here, while I pray.' (John 10:11)

He involved others in the deep places of the soul. They could witness his agony and ecstasy in the presence of God.

- 'He set his face to go to Jerusalem.' (Luke 9:51)

Here was a person with a mission, a sense of purpose, who gave himself for the sake of the master goal.

- 'Pray then like this.' (Matthew 6:9)

Here he was giving directions, instruction and teaching.

- '. . . the Lord appointed seventy others, and sent them on ahead of him, two by two, into every town and place . . .' (Luke 10:1)

He let people discover the work of ministry at first hand. By this they would discover its joys and sorrows, and learn. He gave them freedom to learn.

- 'You are my friends if you do what I command you. No longer do I call you servants . . .' (John 15:14)

Here was fellow-feeling and companionship in the work. Strange as it may seem, Jesus was giving them a sense of equality in the cause.

- 'Go therefore and make disciples of all nations . . .' (Matthew 28:19)

Jesus gave commands, but it was a command to share the work.

- 'But you shall receive power when the Holy Spirit has come upon you, and you shall be my witnesses . . .' (Acts 1:8)

Jesus offers 'empowerment' to his followers to get on with the work, in the power of the Spirit. He released them, with power. Jesus' ministry was marked by a diversity of styles of leadership. Yet it is clear that at the centre was love toward the Father, and love for people. Learning to love will be at the centre of our efforts of leadership. Christian care can temper our inadequecies or our misguided bumptiousness or fear to let go and let others learn too.

3 LEADING THE TEAM

You are the leader of a team whose primary function is to conduct the children's club. But you are also leading a team in which all are on the Christian pilgrimage. The equipping of team members, then, is both for their own spiritual growth as well as for their ministry with children. Whereas other learning programs have attended to the ministry with children, we are now concentrating on the needs of the team. How can you, as leader, consider the needs of the team members?

Let us imagine members are gathering for a meeting of the children's club team. It may be that different concerns are in their minds.

One may think, 'I would like us to plan for a games night, because we have not tried that idea'. Another may think, 'It is very important that we keep this team together, and especially to make Josie feel welcome'. While another may be thinking, 'I hope I am not asked to prepare the worship for the kids; I would shake at the knees!'

As you think about those statements you can recognise three different areas of concern. The first was thinking about tasks to be done; about running the club and its programs. The emphasis was on *task needs*.

The second was thinking about the needs of the club team, where there is a new person, and where there are probably many different ideas about everything. The emphasis for this person was on *building the team* or *group maintenance needs*.

The third was caught up by a personal fear. This person will need encouragement and the development of skill and confidence. That can happen if the team is sensitive. The emphasis for this person was on *individual needs*. It is the need in the team for *developing individuals*.

These three areas of need can be found in any group which is trying to work together. The club leader will benefit by using these three areas of need to recognise concerns from individuals in the team. The areas overlap. Each area needs attention.

Fig. 9:1

We can briefly consider matters to look for in each of the three areas. A leader alert to these by doing some 'inner work' in the mind, will become sensitive to needs and will be able to guide the team in meeting needs.

What is included in *achieving tasks*? The work of planning and running programs will be the main component of this area. Several examples are:

- conducting the regular program
- recruiting children
- arranging for a family night
- planning a camp.

Tasks require planning and co-ordination. The results are easier 'to see' as they are happening.

What is included in *building the team*? Here are some factors which belong to this area of team need:

- setting standards of attendance and sharing responsibility

- maintaining self-discipline
- increasing team morale
- ensuring we have a sense of purpose which is our mission
- giving and sharing of tasks and responsibilities, and learning to do new things to support the team
- communicating with each other
- training each other

What is included in *developing individuals*? Here are some examples of concerns which belong to this area:

- attending to personal problems
- encouraging individuals in the team
- giving status to others
- affirming members in new endeavours
- recognising and using individual abilities
- training the individual members of the team.

For a time, one area could need particular attention. Balance is needed, however, over the long term. To give 'achieving tasks' all the energy would mean that individual's needs for support or guidance could be neglected. Eventually the team could disintegrate if not enough care is given to 'group maintenance — building the team' or to the needs for support or direction for individuals in the area of 'developing individuals'.

What is the skill of the leader? It is recognising the factors that belong to the three areas of group and individual need, as they can be recognised in your team, and influencing the team to meet those needs.

Task

As club leader, are there some particular needs that arise in your mind as you reflect on your team? Try to complete these sentence stubs, and clarify specific tasks and needs.

a. A 'task' I want to achieve in the club is

....

b. A 'building the team' task I want to work on

is..

....

c. A 'developing individuals' task I must

attend to is ....

....

Share your findings with your mentor.

4 TEAM MEMBERS HELPING AND HINDERING TEAM PERFORMANCE

The members of your team will have concerns that are represented by each of the three circles. A team feeling develops when each circle of need is being given attention, as necessary. The style of leadership that you model can show that you are interested in:

- the work of the club being done effectively
- the members of the team enjoying the work and being open with each other, and
- the individuals making progress in their own development.

Your leadership will set the tone. You do not lead alone, however. Each person in the team can contribute to the team goals being achieved. Group accomplishment is helped by individuals' contributions. The leadership is shared. On the other hand, certain types of individual contributions can hinder the effectiveness of the team. Such contributions make effectiveness more difficult to achieve.

Thus we turn to consider *helping* and *hindering* contributions. Any person on the team can be contributing to the progress and well-being of the team and its work. This is a way for the sharing of the leadership. We can think about it this way.

Member contributions that help get the job done: achieving tasks

Consider how helpful these contributions will be to the work of the team when a person is:

- clarifying: stating his/her own views or others' views in a clear way, perhaps by rewording and expanding the comments
- expediting: stimulating the team to take action and make decisions, and showing how
- contributing: putting in new or different ideas to give material for consideration
- giving information: relevant facts are given to help decision making
- seeking information: asking for facts that others may have
- giving opinions: making 'As I see it' statements that put ideas on the table
- seeking opinions: requesting others to offer their opinions, thus helping the discussion to be open
- summarising: drawing ideas and concepts together

- record-keeping: where one offers to keep the notes of the decisions made so that action plans are not forgotten.

To have these contributions coming from team members is to have a positive, shared leadership approach to achieving the club's tasks.

Member contributions needed for group maintenance: building the team

Each member can help to build the team. Consider these contributions. These are like gifts to each other. They are valuable gifts too. It is helpful when members contribute by:

- giving praise: where any member praises ideas or suggestions put forward
- encouraging: where members indicate warm attitudes towards others
- harmonising: drawing different viewpoints together, especially when the common ground is not plain
- observing: noting how the team is working, asking for ideas from quiet members, or noting if the discussion is away from the subject
- standard setting: reminding the team to follow considerate procedures, such as, one speaker at a time
- acknowledging: when a person acknowledges that the discussion has shown that their idea is not the best and asking for it to be withdrawn, so allowing the team to work with the better ideas
- agreeing: saying so when ideas are agreeable
- sensitising: asking the team to give further thought to someone's suggestion which appears to be neglected or ignored
- adding humour: contributing good natured warmth that allows the team to relax, think positively and enjoy working and being together.

Blessed is the team where members learn to share the leadership as they make such team-building contributions.

Members' contributions that reveal individual needs and call for team members' concern and action

There are some contributions that hinder both the task and the team-building aims of the club.

These call for careful treatment by the leader, with the help of others who recognise the personal needs that can lie behind such behaviours. Where members behave in these ways they will hinder the work of the team. Hindrances can be seen when members are:

- dominating: attempting to out-talk or over-talk
- blocking: impeding progress by stubborn or unreasoning resistance
- playboying: clownish horseplay that diverts attention from important work to prevent progress
- seeking sympathy: deprecating oneself in order to turn attention away from the task to oneself
- filibustering: time wasting by raising irrelevant matters.

These are behaviours which hinder rather than help. The people concerned may need firm but gracious control. First, you need to recognise what they are doing and put a name to it in your mind. Second you need to assert your leadership and call the group to its central task. In a mainly healthy team, there will be others too who will support the objectives and press hinderers to become helpers.

You will also encounter other 'individual needs' that are different from the hindering contributions. These behaviours stem from lack of experience, lack of confidence, or low self-esteem. Consider these needs where people are:

- hesitant: where a new experience is required, or a new skill needs to be learned, and the person fills with doubt
- low in confidence: the task is new and the person has not had the necessary experience to be confident in their ability
- incompetent: possibly because of inexperience, or lack of training. Sometimes the task is outside their skill area
- immature: the team member is young and life experience has not prepared him/her for work with children.

These too represent individual needs. The people may be willing to help, but do not know how yet, or may not have had the background experience. They will need caring relationships, and clear directions as they are encouraged to build their experience and their confidence. Your task is to awaken within them 'the children's worker waiting to burst out'.

Team-building will happen as you model helping ways, and as you affirm and praise the helping contributions that come from others. It will happen as you influence hindering behaviour towards more positive contributions. It will happen too as you recognise people's fears and patiently push them into new tasks, supporting them and building their confidence and esteem.

Task

This is a personal reflection task. Think about the people on your club team. Are they, more or less, 'helpers' or 'hinderers' in their participation? Are there some who need:

a. much personal support and large amounts of direction and explanation about what to do
b. much personal support even though they know what they have to do, and can do it
c. little personal support and little direction
d. little personal support and no direction because they know what to do, how to do it, and do not need to be told.

Try to put each person against one of these categories. You do not have to tell anyone of your findings, but the exercise will help you become clear about team members' 'individual needs'.

As the club leader, you have goals for each member of the team. You desire that each one will develop in their competence as leaders. You will desire this for yourself as well. Your example will set the scene for the team.

This philosophy is a useful guide.

Phase 1: I do it, and you watch.

Phase 2: I do it, and you do it.

Phase 3: You do it, and I will support and supervise.

Phase 4: You do it, and I will move on to the next area for learning.

Task

Here are two case studies. You are the leader. Consider which action you would choose. State your choice and expand it with your reasons, in writing. Use your notes in conversation with your mentor.

Case 1.

If an assistant club leader in our club, despite previous requests from me, continued to make distracting remarks to other leaders during meetings I would:

a. Ignore her behaviour as attention seeking.
b. Explain to her the effect her remarks have on others and ask her to be quiet.
c. Tell her to be quiet and get on with her own tasks.
d. Encourage her to discuss any personal problems in order to discover the reason for her behaviour.

Case 2.
If a relatively new assistant leader, after causing difficulty by arriving late two meetings in a row, arrived thirty minutes late on the third occasion, without explanation, I would:
a. Show my disappointment by ignoring him completely.
b. Explain to him that his absence places an unfair load on others and tell him he must come on time.
c. Tell him that you will complain to the Council of Elders.
d. Sit down and listen to his explanation with understanding.

---

5 FEEDBACK — SUPPORT — DIRECTION

A number of your team will be new to club leadership. You may have recruited older teenagers as junior assistants. Sometimes they will be close to the children in many ways, and the children will like them. Sometimes they may behave like big children rather than the young adults you need to rely on. Other assistants may be adults, but who have no experience of club work, and who are required to master new skills.

In any of these cases, your task is to provide your assistants with guidance so that they can contribute to the purposes of the club. And of course, you may be new to the work too. There are ways to proceed, but it will mean giving your low-in-confidence or untried-ability leaders big contributions of your leadership energy.

What does that require? First, they must come to recognise sincere friendship from you. They need to learn that you are trustworthy, and sensitive to their needs. They know, for example, that you will not direct or criticise them in front of the children.

Second, they need to recognise that you know where you are going, and that you have a sense of purpose. You have a vision for the club that you are imparting to them. In that vision are contained achievable standards of leader performance.

Third, they need you to build them up, not knock them down. They will need genuine affirmation. They need to know that you want them to be there.

Fourth, they will need to be given clear and simple directions about what is required. They need time 'to walk things through with you' away from the club. They need to be clear about your expectations.

Fifth, they will need 'feedback' which is affirming and constructive. There are several important points to consider about giving feedback.

1. Feedback should only be attempted when the mood is open and constructive. It can be counter-productive to attempt to give feedback when everyone is 'cranky'.

2. Feedback should only be given when you both have time to talk the matter through. It is unfair to drop a comment and then rush away.

3. Feedback can be acceptable in an atmosphere of mutuality.

4. Feedback needs to be phrased in terms which are reasonable and achievable for that particular person. You should not expect a low-in-confidence leader to be transformed into a highly competent leader in the twinkling of an eye.

5. Feedback is most fruitful when it is asked for. You can set the tone by asking an assistant to observe you in an area of club work and give you comments.

6. Feedback is useful as an aid to learning when it is concentrated on one activity or skill.

Here are three steps to guide you in giving feedback.

Step one: describe and affirm what was commendable about the assistant's performance. 'I liked the way you did that.' 'I thought you introduced that game in a very clear way. The children responded well, didn't they?'

Step two: give 'I' statements about an area of performance where improvement is possible, *but* only if you can phrase suggestions that are achievable for this particular person. 'It seemed to me that some foul-play developed in that game. When that happens, let's not hesitate to stop the game and deal with it. Next time, step in quickly. I'll support you.' 'I noticed the children were not all ready when the Bible reading was begun. I find it useful to pause, and make eye contact with children. Would you be able to practise that too?'

Step three: add a word of praise about a further quality or competence that you noted.

If you frame your feedback comments in 'I' statements, they will be more acceptable to the learner. The learner can accept or reject them. He/she does not need to argue or justify the action. It is a more productive method than statements such as 'You did a crazy thing tonight!' or 'What got into you to do it that way?' Rather you will want to be clear so that the assistant recognises another dimension to the skill they are learning, and caring so that the assistant is assured of your support.

Task

Reflect on the methods you use in giving directions or corrections to your assistants. Can you use these feedback guidelines about giving feedback? Use them in practice. Giving feedback constructively is a personal skill that can improve with practice. It is dependent on sound and trusting relationships, and personal integrity from you. Ask an assistant to give you feedback about an aspect of your work with children. When feedback has mutuality, then the team learn together. Write down three sentences that are your 'learnings' through giving and receiving feedback. Show your sentences and tell your mentor about these feedback experiences.

6 HOW TO SET GOALS

A lively children's club has goals. These are the goals of the leaders, and, in particular, the club leader. The club leader leads the team to set goals, so that they become intentional about their work. They do not see the club as a pastime but rather as an intentional work of ministry for the congregation. The leader of the team helps and fosters the team to set goals. They are able to say, 'We know where we are going!'

Goals bring benefits. Goals provide blueprints for detailed planning, targets for which to aim, and a means for measuring progress. Setting goals is a team process. The vision may come from the leader, or from other members of the team. Discussion is essential in clarifying and defining goals. The leader needs to know how to arrive at a clear, precise goal statement, because the leader will be coaching the team toward goal setting.

Some goal statements can be vague and of little value. 'Sometime we want our club to be bigger' is not a well defined goal statement. It is not clear or precise. A more useful statement would be, 'Our goal is to have thirty child members by August this year; that is to recruit eight new children and one new adult leader'. It is the clear goal statement that will do two things for the team.

One, defining and clarifying goal statements will require discussion, clear thinking and intentional planning.

Two, clear goal statements motivate the team for action. The goal is like the banner under which the team goes to battle.

Features of effective goal statements

Here are five features of goal statements which will serve the club best. The leader can press the team to set goals using these standards.

1. Goals are clear statements. Vague statements make planning difficult. Rather specific terms, precise figures, set dates and actual names are used. All the members know what the goal is because it is stated clearly. Clear goals avoid sometime, somebody and somewhere terms.

2. Goals should be described using quantity and quality terms. A goal can set a figure on how many new members, how much money or how many leaders. It can talk about quality factors, such as recruiting of 'teenage' leaders, or 'adult' leaders or 'craft' helpers. Quantity and quality terms mean the goal can be more readily understood.

3. Goals should be capable of measurement. Because the statement is specific, with details, it can be seen whether the results will be or have been achieved in full, in part, or not at all.

4. Goals should be both attainable and reasonable. A goal should have some challenge to it, but it needs to be set in terms that can be reached. There will be effort required, but the goal is achievable.

5. Goals should have a sensible time span. Both

clear starting dates and a sensible completion date aid planning. Large goals can be broken down into sub-goals if need be.

The club leader in leading the team into setting goals will bring the team to an intentional planning commitment.

Notice the difference

Here are several goal statements. Some of these fit the standards, some do not. Notice, however, how clear and precise some are.

- This hall needs extra toilet facilities.
- Sometime this year we should have a dress-up program.
- Before December this year, this club should have twenty-five members. A recruitment program will begin on 1 August. A dress-up program will be the celebration on attainment of the goal.
- Will somebody please clean up the kitchen?
- Let us have a fete!
- On 10 November the club will conduct an open night for members, parents and families, and people of the congregation. The program will include games for all ages (Cath to organise), three items by the club (Bill and Jane to prepare), a visiting chalk artist (Peter to approach J. Williamson) and supper (bring a plate; Jill and James to co-ordinate). Involving children in the planning will begin on 16 August.

Task

Look over the current plans and programs in your club. Select one of these and write it in a goal statement so that it is clearly stated, in a measurable form, with a reasonable target, and a sensible time span. Show your statement to your mentor. Did you find that by doing this exercise you had to think in more definite and precise terms? Clear goals help the club progress and achieve worthwhile targets.

7 HOW TO PLAN

Planning is the process of thinking ahead. Planning is decision-making about the what, why, when, who, where and how of an event. Planning takes thought. Stating goals is the beginning of planning.

Effective planning means that tasks are

identified beforehand and dealt with gradually and methodically. The consequence of good planning will be well-conducted events that have quality about them. The events will have extras built into them because proper care has been taken in preparation. Poor or haphazard planning results in events where people will say, 'I wish we had thought of this or that!' or another will say, 'We should have included A and B, as well'.

What are the guidelines for planning?

Step one: Define the final event in precise terms. State the goal. What is it that is to be done, and when? Write the goal down. Spend time in discussion, becoming clear about the goal.

Step two: Think of all the jobs that have to be done to get ready for the event, and make notes about these.

Step three: Determine what sequence is required; some tasks must be done before others can be tackled.

Step four: Draw a time-line chart marked out in weeks, showing dates, and the date of the final event. This can be done on a butchers' paper chart, or on a white board.

A time-line chart is set out in Figure 9:2.

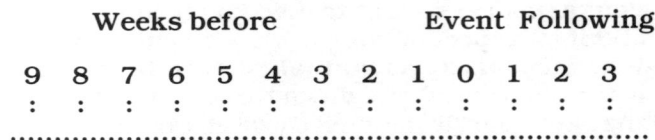

	Weeks before									Event	Following		
9	8	7	6	5	4	3	2	1	0	1	2	3

Particular tasks are written in to be achieved at the appropriate times

Fig. 9:2

Step five: Write on your time-line chart when particular tasks in preparation need to be completed. Comments such as 'book hall', 'design publicity posters', 'print posters', 'prepare publicity for church bulletin' and so on, are written in. The chart may look like a scribbling pad, but the complexities of the arrangements are being thought about, planned and executed piece by piece.

Step six: At the same time consider the resources you will need, such as money, people, materials and space. Find these before you need them.

Step seven: Adjust your planning and your schedules as jobs are done, and write in new ones as they occur. This is often where the final event is improved through people raising ideas well beforehand.

Step eight: Reach your target.

Step nine: De-brief. Make sure all the people are thanked. Check whether your goal was met in all respects. Keep notes for future reference.

Can planning be done in the head? Rarely. Much of the club planning work is done by use of a planner and the written program book. (Refer Chapter 6 'Conducting children's club programs' for information about these.) But complex events, such as a combined clubs event, or a children's club camp, require careful, methodical and documented planning. A club concert, or a fete, or the club attendance at kid's campout are each events with many complexities. For these the time-line approach to planning will help you stage a quality event. Planning ensures that the thinking is done before it is too late to act. Planning is team activity. The team work together. They brainstorm ideas. Jobs will be shared around. The leader co-ordinates and ensures the time-line chart has all the jobs and steps marked on it. Progress is checked regularly.

Task

Try out a time-line plan for an event lying ahead. Plan as a team and fill out your time-line chart showing what jobs will have to be done, and when. The target date needs to have a goal statement with it (how many children, how many helpers, place, etc.)
Show your time-line chart to your mentor.

---

8 RECRUITING LEADERS FOR THE CLUB

Recruitment requires asking. The important factor is to know the type of person who should be asked, the job the person is being asked to do, and the particular person who should be asked.

Recruitment for a church club is the responsibility of the elders, or other such council of the congregation. In reality, however, the club leader will have an important function in pointing out needs, and prompting the necessity of recruitment of suitable persons.

Recruitment is best approached as a group

effort, especially for key leadership positions. Here is a panel approach to the recruitment of leaders that is methodical, and aims to recruit a chosen person to join the club team.

A panel method for recruiting key leaders

The method takes six steps.

Step one: a recruiting panel is formed. A parent, the minister, an elder, and a member of the congregation and yourself could make up the panel. The panel need to know how many people are to be recruited, and what roles they are required to fill.

Step two: The panel will begin looking at two sets of details:
a. what skills are needed for the roles.
b. what personal qualities persons would need to be suited to the tasks. The panel may decide, for example, that they are looking for a person who:
   ● is the kind of person whose influence on our children we could accept with complete confidence
   ● has a strong Christian faith
   ● likes children, and has empathy with them
   ● has leadership qualities or potential
   ● is dependable
   ● can give some time
   ● is a team person
   ● is willing to be trained
   ● is liked by children
   ● has acceptance with parents
   ● is part of the congregation
   ● is likely to see the task as ministry for the Lord to children.

The panel thus works out the type of person required.

Step three: A brainstorming approach is taken to listing all the possible names known to the members. The panel range over all the contacts they can recall and add names of people who might be suitable. The next task is to draw up a rating grid as described in Figure 9:3 to help in the process of deciding who are the most suitable to be approached.

On the grid will be marked the names of people who have been suggested. Along the top of the grid will be a selection of categories, such as 'Christian faith', 'likes children', 'congregation', 'team person', and 'previous experience'. The panel scores the grid by using 'ticks' in the columns. Two 'ticks' can be used when a person is known to be outstanding in any category. The scores are added. This is a mechanism for sorting and an aid to the panel reaching consensus about the order of preference. The panel will not know about the availability or willingness of the people listed.

	Positive Influence	Christian Faith	Likes Children	Children's attitude to	Team person	Acceptance by parents	Belongs to congregation	Call of the Lord	Score
Agnes Pritchard	✓	✓	✓			✓	✓		5
James Brown		✓				✓	✓		3
Reg Hildetch	✓	✓	✓✓	✓✓	✓	✓	✓	✓	10
Aileen Trott	✓✓	✓✓	✓	✓✓	✓	✓✓	✓	✓	12
Elizabeth Bond	✓	✓	✓	?	?	?		✓	4

Fig. 9:3

At the end of *step three* a list of names can be made with the most desired name at the top. Some names will be considered not suitable for the position and these will not be pursued. Of course, this is a confidential process and the panel will not disclose its discussion.

Step four: The next step is to plan the approach. 'We want to ask in the best way we can for this person to join the leadership team. We want to show that we believe he/she is the right person for this position. How can we do that in the best way?' The panel also decides on who will make the approach. This is best done by a spokesperson with two others.

Step five: The panel spokesperson makes an appointment for a meeting in the person's home. The prospect's spouse is invited to participate.

Step six: the panel spokesperson and supporters call on the prospect. The spokesperson explains to the prospect:

- why he/she is being approached
- exactly what it is you want the person to do.

In the conversation, the visiting panel members will want to show clearly:

- that you believe the person is the right person for the position
- that this decision to ask was made with great care and prayer
- that you will respect their decision
- that you want to be clear about explaining the requirements and commitments involved.

Although pressure should not be applied, the visitors need to show that they are deliberate, intentional and enthusiastic in the task of locating the most suitable leaders for the club. If the person asks for time to consider, then arrange for a suitable day and hour for the spokesperson to make contact again.

If the person agrees, then the club leader has an immediate task of settling in the new person and giving him/her the particular tasks.

If the person declines, then the spokesperson and supporters will arrange to meet the next person on their list.

Recruiting resource helpers

The children's club needs to have access to resource helpers. These are people who come from time to time to support the club in some way. The learning program on 'administration' describes the use of a parent survey form which is completed at the time of a child's enrolment. Such a form is found in Chapter 5, page 44. Parents will be a major source of resource helpers.

The parent survey indicates categories of support which parents, or other members of the congregation, may be able to offer the club. Resource people can assist:

- with transport
- with supervision
- as a leader, helper or instructor
- with money raising
- with outings, or trips, or camps
- with occasional suppers
- children to learn about their own hobbies, work, skills, sports or interests.

If you use this parent survey over time, you will build up a list of people who will support the work and programs of the club, as they are invited.

Along with the parent survey method, two others can be listed. One is through long term planning, recognising the type of resource help you will need, and advertising for helpers in the congregation. The other is by keeping your eyes and ears open amongst the congregation and your other contacts, and so discovering the interests, activities or pastimes which people follow. You then keep a note with your parent survey forms. After gaining people's interest in helping, you should be specific in asking them to help at a particular meeting. Avoid asking but never using. Keep the lists alive, and use people as often as you can. From your resource helpers list may come those who will join the club team.

Task

What is your situation? Is there a major recruitment task lying ahead? What steps will you take to encourage the congregation to meet the need?
Do you have a current resource helpers list? If not, is it time to begin this aspect of the work? Describe your plans concerning recruitment of key adults and resource helpers to your mentor.

9 RESOURCES

Two titles explore leadership more deeply. They are: John Adair, *Effective Leadership: A Modern Guide to Developing Leadership Skills* (London: Pan Books, 1983) and, Kenneth Blanchard, Patricia Zigarmi and Drea Zigarmi, *Leadership and the One Minute Manager* (London: Willow Books, 1985.)
Other titles in the 'One Minute Manager' series could also be useful. Perhaps your church library will have copies which you may borrow.

10 DRAWING IT TOGETHER

In this learning program we have seen the importance of the three areas of need. The diagram of the three over-lapping circles is a symbol of the needs to be met by the club team. These are:

- achieving tasks
- building the team, maintaining the group

- meeting individual needs and developing individuals in their skills.

As leader, you can encourage the team to meet those needs. It will take energy and sensitivity. But by your modelling you will show how you desire the team to contribute and care for each other, while doing the work together.

Here is a summary of how the team can operate. This represents a highly significant goal to be achieved. Your goal for the team can be outlined this way.

What is the basis for decisions in the team? It is by discussion and agreement.

What are the forms of control on the team? These are established through sharing and caring relationships, and commitments to the work and each other.

What is the source of power in the team? The team is undergirded by the power of the Spirit, and it finds its power in what 'we' think and feel. The team 'feels' group support.

What is the desired end of the team's discussion? It is consensus, support for the aims, purposes and methods of the club worked out together.

What is to be stressed in the club? There will be a need for you to act as the designated leader at times, especially where on-the-spot decisions are required. But the stress will be on shared leadership and mutual goal setting, in which you take an energetic and constructive part.

How are team members to regard each other? It is most desirable that despite differences of age or experience, the team members learn to regard each other as peers, as fellow workers.

How are relationships shaped? They are not to be seen as structured in an hierarchical manner, nor on the other hand seen merely as a collection of individuals each doing their own thing. Rather the team is group-oriented establishing its relationships in a fellowship of Christian workers with fellow-feeling.

What is the basis for personal growth? It is not ultimately based on sergeant/soldier or lecturer/student dealings, but rather on peer group membership, where members are helped to care for and learn from each other.

These factors may not be a description of your team at this moment. As the leader with the insight, you will be able with patience and energy to accentuate the sharing of leadership.

You will model this style. Your goal will be to develop a team which:

- gets the work done
- builds itself in morale and Christian grace
- develops the individuals in their confidence and competence.

Put simply, the stages we desire will be:

Stage 1 I am the designated leader.

Stage 2 I am the designated leader but I share the leadership with others.

Stage 3 We are the leaders and we share the work together.

Stage 4 From the team a new designated leader arises.

Stage 5 The new designated leader shares the leadership with others.

Stage 6 We are the leaders and we share the work together.

If you have that vision to help the assistants and helpers become a team, and that goal is achieved, then a true ministry team for the congregation is established. The team members will gain, but more importantly, so will the children of the club.

SELF-ASSESSMENT

When you have completed the tasks outlined in this program, you will be ready for this assessment activity with the aid of your mentor.

It is a joint activity, with conversation, through which your mentor will endorse the completion of the tasks. The mentor will be looking at the shared leadership practices in the club, and helping you assess whether you have contributed the appropriate leadership functions according to the needs of the team. The mentor will be able to give you feedback on team morale as he/she sees it. These conversations will be useful as you develop in your leadership.

Levels of performance: Place an 'X' in the appropriate box. If, because of special circumstances, a component was not applicable, or impossible to execute, an 'X' may be placed in the 'not applicable' box. All items should receive a n/a, good or excellent response. If any item receives a none, poor or fair response, then you and the mentor will need to determine what additional activities are required in order to complete that component. It may mean improving methods to gain further team involvement, and then inviting your mentor to observe and discuss further the measures you are taking. The aim is for the team to be giving attention to each of the three circles of need: achieving tasks, building the team and group maintenance, and meeting individual needs and developing individuals.

		N/A	None	Poor	Fair	Good	Excellent
1	As leader, I state a club goal which has the features:						
a.	stated clearly	☐	☐	☐	☐	☐	☐
b.	stated in measurable terms	☐	☐	☐	☐	☐	☐
c.	sets reasonable/ achievable targets	☐	☐	☐	☐	☐	☐
d.	sets sensible time span.	☐	☐	☐	☐	☐	☐
2	As leader, I name one current 'task' goal.	☐	☐	☐	☐	☐	☐
3	As leader, I name one current 'team-building' goal.	☐	☐	☐	☐	☐	☐
4.	As leader, I name one current 'individual development' goal.	☐	☐	☐	☐	☐	☐
5	As leader, I can name a suitable successor and have begun training that person.	☐	☐	☐	☐	☐	☐
6	As leader, I provide direction and personal support, as appropriate to varying situations such as:						
a.	direct, tactful guidance to immature assistants	☐	☐	☐	☐	☐	☐
b.	giving mature assistants freedom to act	☐	☐	☐	☐	☐	☐

	N/A	None	Poor	Fair	Good	Excellent

c. supporting assistants with personal attention. ☐☐☐☐☐☐

7 As leader, I act as pastor to assistants and helpers by:

a. praying for them ☐☐☐☐☐☐

b. developing their abilities ☐☐☐☐☐☐

c. training them to accept increased responsibility ☐☐☐☐☐☐

d. affirming them in their faith ☐☐☐☐☐☐

e. taking/enrolling them in training events ☐☐☐☐☐☐

f. supporting each other in worship attendance ☐☐☐☐☐☐

g. meeting with them as a team at least bi-monthly ☐☐☐☐☐☐

h. modelling open communication ☐☐☐☐☐☐

i. seeking feedback from a team member ☐☐☐☐☐☐

j. offering feedback in an appropriate manner, to individual team members ☐☐☐☐☐☐

k. meeting with the team socially on occasions. ☐☐☐☐☐☐

8 As leader, I attend training events for personal development at least twice a year. ☐☐☐☐☐☐

9 As leader, I use a time-line approach to planning events and submit a plan for an upcoming event. ☐☐☐☐☐☐

10 As leader, I employ a panel approach to recruitment of assistants and helpers. ☐☐☐☐☐☐

Mentor's endorsement

I declare that (leader's name) .... has completed the self-assessment tasks of this learning program with good or excellent markings.

Signed.................................. (mentor).........(date)

Chapter 10

The learning process — individual and small group

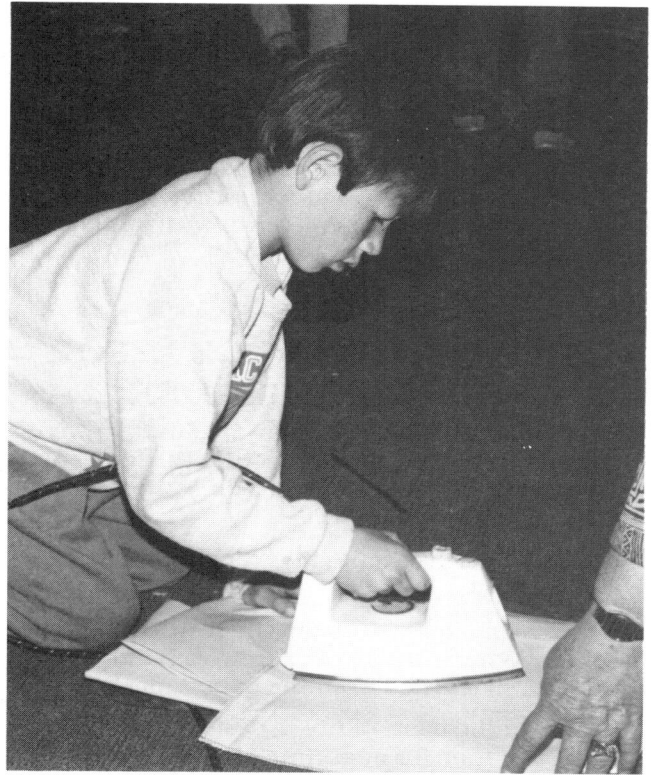

The learning programs in the chapters of Part 2 — Process have been designed on three key principles. Ministers, elders, trainers or mentors who have responsibility for equipping club leaders will find that an understanding of these principles will enhance the learner-leader's gains from involvement in these programs.

FIRST PRINCIPLE

The most important tasks for a club leader are those that are central to the job. What does the leader have to do? The content of the programs is based on research that set out to specifically identify the essential tasks of a club leader. The research had two phases.[1]

Phase One brought together a number of club leaders, assistants, helpers, parents and ministers who listed all the tasks, jobs and responsibilities that a club leader is to fulfil. The lengthy list was then focused into specific statements.

Phase Two was to submit a marking sheet to the people from Phase One, and others as well, who marked each task in terms of 'importance' and 'learning difficulty'. These markings were then collated to give a clear indication of the 'highly important' and 'difficult to learn' tasks. These tasks feature on the self-assessment pages of each learning program.

The learning programs thus concentrate on the essential, significant and central tasks that a club leader needs to master.

SECOND PRINCIPLE

The tasks need to be performed competently. If the centrally important tasks can be done well, then many less important tasks will flow on.

99

THIRD PRINCIPLE

The only way a leader can show competent performance is on the job — on the church hall floor as it were. Can the leader do it? Can the leader be observed using improved skill? It is not just 'reading about' or 'knowing about' a subject; it is whether the leader can perform that work, task, skill or activity competently with children in the club.

THE LEARNING PROCESS FOR THE INDIVIDUAL LEADER

For the individual the maximum gain from using the learning programs will occur if the 'do, look, think, grow' process is valued. This process can be described this way.

Do: The leader tries out ideas, practices, experiences.

Look: The leader reflects on the results. What worked? What didn't work? How well did I do? What have I learned from the experience?

Think: On the basis of my experiences, what should I change for next time? How should I do it differently? The leader becomes clear about the things that do not need to change, as well as the changes that will bring improvement in their performance.

Grow: I do it better now. Through the experience and the self-assessment, I can be more competent. I can now do it well and effectively.

This cycle of learning is a feature of these learning programs.

The learning programs use three approaches to encourage the 'do, look, think, grow' process.

1. Brief reading material, with guidelines for action in the various tasks of leadership.

2. Learning tasks: exercises within the program to encourage reflection, conversation and action

3. Self-assessment exercises that outline the significant tasks; and are carried out with a mentor.

THE KEY ROLE OF THE MENTOR

The mentor is an 'aide-to-learning', a 'friend-on-the-way' who will assist the learning process as a supporter, encourager and observer.

The essence of this approach is that the club leader is to show competent performance of the respective tasks which the position entails. Learning is seen to be accomplished *if* the club leader carries out each task at an adequate level of performance, in practice at club meetings and activities.

The mentor's function is to help the club leader assess his/her actual performance against a stated standard. To do this, the mentor will be an observer of the leader at work.

The mentor will become involved in self-assessment discussions with the club leader. This process has the potential to be a powerful learning experience, subject to two things happening.

First, the club leader accepts a commitment to meet the standard, desiring to learn and perform the work with increasing skill, rather than have 'it will do' or 'near enough is good enough' attitudes.

Second, the mentor takes the work of observation seriously, and works at being a helpful interpreter of the standards expected. The particular skill of giving feed-back is significant to the mentor's role.

In short, the mentor will be:

- an observer of the club leader, the club team, and the club in action
- the giver of feedback to the club leader
- a counsellor where the club leader is missing the mark
- a stimulator who, rather than providing ready-made ideas, helps the club leader generate ideas. The mentor points the leader to other parts of the learning programs, or by suggestion awakens the leader to other people or book resources to help the solving of problems
- an asker of questions, rather than a giver of answers
- an encourager where a club leader grows weary, loses heart or feels defeated (children can be trying at times even to the most experienced of leaders)
- a standard bearer prompting improvement where inadequate performance has been the norm. A leader taking over a club accustomed to mediocrity may not realise the potential for improvement unless helped to see the possibilities.

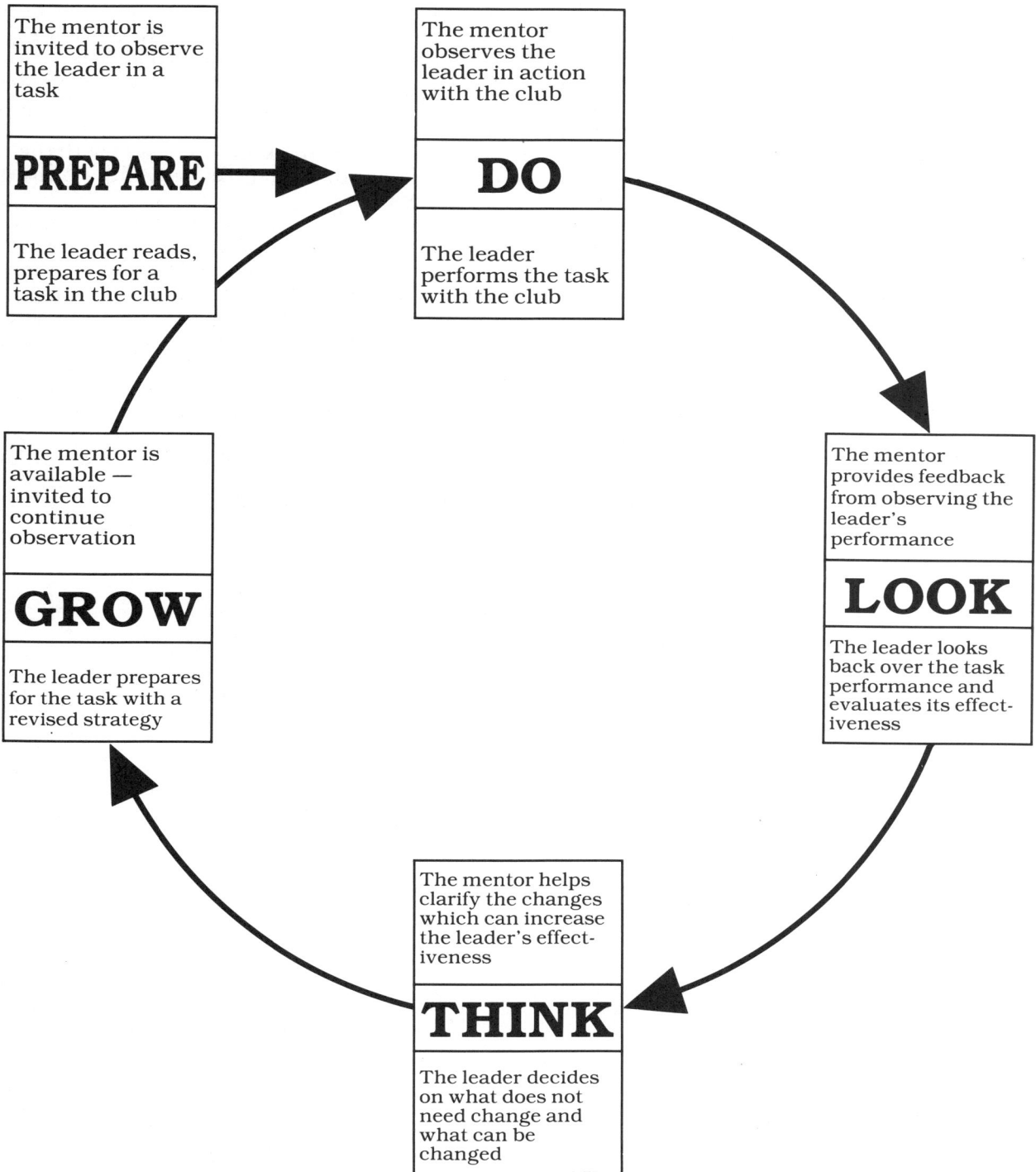

The mentor is invited to observe the leader in a task

PREPARE

The leader reads, prepares for a task in the club

The mentor observes the leader in action with the club

DO

The leader performs the task with the club

The mentor is available — invited to continue observation

GROW

The leader prepares for the task with a revised strategy

The mentor provides feedback from observing the leader's performance

LOOK

The leader looks back over the task performance and evaluates its effectiveness

The mentor helps clarify the changes which can increase the leader's effectiveness

THINK

The leader decides on what does not need change and what can be changed

DO   LOOK   THINK   GROW

Fig. 10:1

But what if a club leader chooses a mentor who is not well-acquainted with children's club work? The mentor is not intended to provide expert direction and be an encyclopaedia of information. Rather, the mentor is to be the outside pair of eyes who observes and interprets whether the standards are being achieved. Such a person will make a valuable contribution, not through being or not being an expert, but from drawing attention to the levels of accomplishment that will bring benefit to the club.

How can a mentor be equipped to take up the role? On being approached to become a mentor, a person should be given the opportunity to do two things before agreeing. The two actions are:

First, to read the 'Open Letter to Mentors' which is found in the next chapter. This letter describes the task of mentoring, and in particular gives guidance about giving feedback.

Second, to read, if possible, several of the learning programs in order to gain an overview of the tasks. A mentor would need to have a copy of the learning programs, of course. When agreeing, the mentor would need to read carefully the learning program the leader had decided to commence.

WORKING WITH A SMALL GROUP

These are programs for individual learning. But in many churches it will be appropriate for the Council of Elders to foster the use of these programs for the in-service training of its children's club team.

Leaders who have been on the job for a time, and leaders who are less experienced could well be brought together to use this training approach. The group could be convened, for example, by the elder responsible for children's ministry, who could act as convener and mentor to the members of the team.

Many of the learning tasks could be dealt with as part of training night programs. Discussion can be shared. Ideas and tasks could be practised amongst each other.

In the end, however, each individual could only satisfy the self-assessment standards if he/she had been observed performing these tasks with the club. That means the mentor must observe competent performance at the club itself.

This method will mean that although much training work can be done in the small group, the individuals may be tackling different parts of the learning programs at any one time. The mentor's observing eye may then have to range over several leaders on the same occasion, as for example, one tells the story, another leads a game and another plans and explains an outreach project. The feedback conversations to follow should be handled with each individual as they evaluate their own performance. There will be occasions when group discussion with the mentor about the general effectiveness of the club may be beneficial.

Some congregations will purchase copies of *Leading a kids club in your church* for their church library. The self-assessment pages have had copyright restrictions removed to allow photo-copying of these pages for the individual leader's use. The leader can have the benefit of a personal self-assessment record, and the unmarked copy remains available to others.

The method underlying these learning programs relies on a leader and a mentor being prepared to work together around the essential tasks of club leadership. The mentor's role is significant. In the next chapter, the mentor's role is outlined further in an open letter.

Note

1. The research methodology and tabulations are fully described in V. J. Cracknell, 'Self-directed learning programs for leaders of Church children's Clubs', submitted to Fuller Theological Seminary as a dissertation, 1988.

Chapter 11

Open letter to mentors

You have been asked to be a mentor for a church children's club leader who needs some help in using a self-directed learning program.

We hope you can agree, but before you do, you will find it helpful to read this letter carefully to gain insight into the mentor's role. You will also find it useful to look at some of the material that the club leader will be using.

WHAT ARE THE CLUB LEADER'S LEARNING PROGRAMS DESIGNED TO DO?

They are firstly designed to help inexperienced leaders move into club leadership, and to help them develop skills in working with children. The learning programs concentrate on the individual tasks that leadership of a club requires. The programs do not stress the learning of theory, but rather the carrying out of the functions of leadership in the club.

FOUR FACETS OF THE MENTOR'S ROLE

a) Observation

The mentor observes what is happening in the club, and 'sees' the leader performing the tasks of leadership. Is the leader conducting games with control, or enrolling children, or using permit forms for the protection of children?

b) Comparison

The mentor observes the club leader in action, performing the functions of leadership. The mentor compares the leader's performance with the task standards set out in the self-assessment statements at the end of each learning program. These statements are set in measurable terms.

Mentors should be able to say in their minds: 'I have seen the leader do that task, but he/she needs more practice in order to meet the standards in the self-assessment list'.

c) Interpretation

The Mentor compares the leader's performance against a stated standard, and arrives at a personal view about the leader's progress in meeting the standard.

d) Feedback

Feedback includes praising, affirming and applauding. It means also indicating learning gaps and suggesting possible alternatives to the leader. Sometimes it will mean asking for a further occasion to observe. The mentor's feedback needs to be encouraging so that the new leader gains confidence as new skills are attempted and eventually mastered.

TWO SEGMENTS IN EACH LEARNING PROGRAM

When you read Part 2 of this book, you will realise that the mentor will be involved in two key areas.

LEARNING TASKS

As leaders read through the material, they are set certain learning tasks. For example, on p. 53 the leader is to choose a song, teach it and ask the mentor to observe and give feedback on an aspect of the task with the club. On p. 40 the leader is asked to mock-up a design for a publicity poster, and to discuss the design with the mentor.

Sometimes the learning tasks are personal and do not have to be discussed with the mentor. Page 65 contains a personal exercise where the leader is asked to look through the club roll and picture each child. If the leader wishes to share discoveries from such a personal exercise then the mentor will also benefit from the conversation.

The learning tasks, then, in the main require the leader to discuss issues or show materials to the mentor. All these are designed to increase a leader's competence in the essential tasks of serving effectively in a children's club.

SELF-ASSESSMENT CONVERSATIONS

The other significant segment in each learning program lies in the self-assessment pages at the end of each program. After working through all the program contents and applying each task practically in the club, the leader is asked to discuss their self-assessment gradings with you as mentor. You will have observed them in action in the club. Perhaps in giving feedback you have already encouraged further practice in some area.

If a leader is competent and you have observed the effectiveness of the leader's performance of a task, then you proceed to suggest a 'good' or 'excellent' marking. Where you believe more practice is required, you indicate that you want to delay marking until the leader has had some more practice. Then when you are both assured that a satisfactory standard has been reached, you suggest that the marking of 'good' or 'excellent' be made. Your desire is that the leader will want to accomplish the best of which they are capable.

The self-assessment process for a learning program concludes when you both agree that all the tasks are being performed competently, and each task has been given a grading. You then sign off the learning program and congratulate the leader (and yourself) on work well done. You then ask the leader which of the remaining learning programs is relevant to tackle next.

Perhaps there are some other questions in your mind. Here are some questions and answers which may cover points you are raising.

What if the leader is missing the mark?
There may be occasions when the leader
- grows weary, feels defeated or is frustrated
- is accustomed to inadequate performance with inadequate standards
- is low in confidence because of lack of experience.

On such occasions the mentor will need to be tactful and encouraging but prepared to insist that a higher standard in some task is possible and desirable. Most of us need practice and experience in order to learn how to do better.

What if the leader needs further training?
The mentor may recognise that the leader could benefit from attendance at a course or training event, to be conducted by the church or other agency. Such suggestions can be made. It is part of the mentoring role.

What if the mentor considers the leader is not performing to the desired standard in a particular task?

Tactful feedback is required. Small steps need to be suggested so that the leader gradually gains confidence and skill.

How does the mentor know if the leader is performing to the desired standard?

You will find a set of statements in the self-assessment pages of each learning program. These represent observable measures. Can you see these things happening in the club? Is there evidence before your eyes? Is the leader actually doing, or causing to be done, what each statement describes? Look for quality and quantity terms. Is the leader meeting these? Look back to the text of the learning program. Does that give you more of the flavour of the task and the standard of performance required? These are the comparing and interpreting aspects of the mentor's role. You do need to be satisfied that the leader has now reached a good or excellent performance.

How do you arrive at the markings?

This is done through conversation. On the one hand, the leader has a fair idea about how his/her performance is going in regard to particular tasks. On the other hand, you have insights because of your observation, comparison and interpretation and you are in a position to give feedback. The process of feedback will be acceptable in such conversation. Some guidelines about feedback are provided below.

You can suggest not declaring a mark at any point because of the need for more practice. You will want to be able to suggest honest 'good' or 'excellent' markings because you have observed that level of performance.

What about a leader who underestimates his/ her performance?

There are perfectionists who set themselves a high standard in all they do. They may be very mindful of the imperfections. Your task, if they have performed at an adequate level according to the standards set, is to press for the appropriate marking and encourage them to keep on with their work, always open to new learning.

What about a leader who overestimates the level of his/her performance?

Some will be:

● over confident, but not sensitive to the need for improvement

● 'anything goes' leaders who are satisfied with mediocrity

● 'always done it this way' people who are not aware of the possibilities for improvement.

A leader of any of these types will need tactful but firm feedback that indicates to them that they can expect more of themselves, that task performance can be of higher standard, and that the life of the club will benefit if their performance is raised.

Will some conversations be painful?

Most new learning has some pain about it especially if we are confronted by new learnings about ourselves. But learning is beneficial if we find satisfaction, find the tasks easier to do, or see some improvement as a result. In a painful conversation, it is important to provide well phrased feedback, and to stay with the person long enough to share understandings until each is at ease.

What guidance is there on giving feedback?

It will be simpler for both if there is an understanding about the particular tasks to be discussed. The leader may indicate this by specifying the work which has been done and for which they feel ready for the self-assessment process.

Because of this forewarning (even though you will have had your 'observation' faculties in tune all the time) you can be ready to take the four steps of observation, comparison, interpretation and then feedback.

There are three steps in giving feedback.

Step one: Describe and affirm what was commendable about the leader's performance. Say clearly what you liked about the way in which the task was handled.

Step two: Give 'I' statements about an area of performance where improvement is possible but only if you can provide suggestions that are achievable for this particular person.

Step three: Add a word of praise about a further quality or competence that you noted.

In giving feedback, there needs to be a balance between highlighting things that are right, as well as suggesting lines of change.

Why use 'I' statements in giving feedback?

An 'I' statement is one in which you state your observation. 'It appeared to me that . . .' 'The impression I gained was . . .' 'I sensed that the quiet game caused difficulty because . . .' These statements allow the leader to hear how an observer perceived the action. Such statements have greater acceptability than those which seem to lay blame on the leader and where the mentor may appear to be a judge.

The learner hears your comment about how you saw or experienced the action. Because it is 'your' observation, the leader does not have to argue about accepting or rejecting the comment.

This approach is more conducive to acceptance of suggestions for gaining more experience, or some further practice, or to lifting the standard of performance in a relevant direction.

CONCLUSION

The children's club leader using these learning programs is embarking on a plan to 'learn the job while doing it'. The information in the programs gives essential clues. But the programs cannot provide the extra and outside set of eyes which could be of benefit to the learner leader.

And that is why you have been asked to be a mentor. I hope you can find it possible to say 'yes'. It will take some time. It will require careful thinking.

The results will be considerable in the benefits brought to the life of the chidren's club. The value to the learner leader from your involvement will be considerable.

May the Lord bless you both as you embark on this partnership of learning.

Useful books and references

There is a wealth of material available on various areas of church life and children's work. The following titles are either mentioned in the text, or may be suggested for those who wish to read more widely. The list is not exhaustive.

BIBLE AND STORY TELLING

Alexander, David and Pat. *The Lion Handbook to the Bible*. Herts. UK: Lion Publishing, (1973) 1981.

Griggs, Patricia. *Using Story Telling in Christian Education*. Melbourne. JBCE, 1981.

Gobbel, Roger and Gobbel, Gertrude. *The Bible — A Child's Playground*. London: SCM Press, 1986.

Stewart, Stan and Hubner, Pauline. *Talking about something important*. Melbourne: JBCE, 1981.

CHILDREN IN THE CHURCH AND CHILDREN'S MINISTRY

Bensen, Denniss C.; Stewart, Stan. J. *The Ministry of the Child*. Nashville: Abingdon, 1979.

British Council of Churches Consultative Group on Ministry among Children. *The Child in the Church*. Reports of the Working Parties on The Child in the Church and Understanding Christian Nurture. British Council of Churches, 1984.

Grierson, Denham. *Focus on the Child*. Melbourne: Dove Communications, 1979.

Richards, Lawrence O. *A New Face for the Church*. Grand Rapids: Zondervan Publishing, 1970.

--------. *A Theology of Christian Education*. Grand Rapids: Zondervan Publishing, 1975.

--------. *A Theology of Children's Ministry*. Grand Rapids: Zondervan Publishing, 1983.

Weber, Hans-Reudi. *Jesus and the Children*. Atlanta: John Knox, 1979.

CHILD DEVELOPMENT

Cully, Iris V. *Christian Child Development*. Melbourne: JBCE, 1979.

Holt, John. *How Children Learn*. Middlesex: Penguin Books, 1973.

Hurlock, Elizabeth. *Child Development*. Sydney: McGraw-Hill, 1978.

Lefrancois, Guy R. *Of Children*. Calif.: Wadsworth Publishing Co., 1977.

Piaget, Jean. *The Child's Conception of the World*. St. Albans, Herts.: Paladin, (1929) 1977.

--------. *The Moral Judgment of the Child*. Middlesex: Penguin Books, 1932.

Scharf, Peter (ed.). *Readings in Moral Education*. Minneapolis: Winston Press, 1978.

Wadsworth, Barry J. *Piaget's Theory of Cognitive Development*. New York: David McKay Co. Inc., 1971.

Wilson, John. *A Teacher's Guide to Moral Education*. London: Geoffrey Chapman, 1973.

CHILDREN'S PARTICULAR NEEDS

Carothers, James E.; Gasten, Ruth. *Helping Children to like themselves. Activities for building self-esteem.* Livermore, Calif.: R/J Associates, (1978), 1981.

Glasser, William. *Schools without failure.* New York: Harper and Row, 1969.

McGinnis, Kathleen and McGinnis, James. *Parenting for Peace and Justice.* New York: Orbis Books, 1985.

Pringle, Mia Kelmer. *The Needs of Children.* London: Hutchinson and Co. Ltd., 1977.

Van Ornum, William, and Murdock, John B. *Crisis Counselling with Children and Adolescents.* New York: Continuum, 1983.

Van Ornum, William and Van Ornum, Mary Whicker. *Talking to Children about Nuclear War.* New York: Continuum Publishing Co., 1984.

Wilt, Joy. *Raising your children toward emotional and spiritual maturity.* Waco: Word Books, 1980.

CLUB ADMINISTRATION

Hunter, Margaret. *Finances Handbook. Budgets, Records and Reports for Small Groups.* Adelaide: S.A. Council of Social Service, 1981.

--------. *Planning Handbook. Planning and Review for Small Groups.* Adelaide: S.A. Council for Social Service, 1981.

CHURCH AS COMMUNITY

Bonhoeffer, Dietrich. *Life Together. A Discussion of Christian Fellowship.* San Francisco: Harper and Row, 1954.

Hauerwas, Stanley. *A Community of Character. Toward a constructive Christian social ethic.* London: University of Notre Dame Press, 1981.

Neville, Gwen Kennedy; Westerhoff, John, III. *Learning through Liturgy.* Melbourne: Dove Communications, 1978.

Ng, David; Thomas, Virginia. *Children in the Worshipping Community.* Atlanta: John Knox Press, 1981.

Nichols, Alan; Clarke, Joan; Hogan, Trevor. *Transforming Families and Communities. Christian Hope in a World of Change.* Sydney: Anglican Consultative Council, 1987.

Stedman, Ray C. *Body Life.* California: Regal Books, (1972), 1986.

Stewart, Stan, with Stewart, Pauline and Green, Richard. *Going to Church with Children.* Melbourne: JBCE, 1989.

Westerhoff, John H.. III. *Will our Children have Faith?* Melbourne: Dove Communications, 1976.

--------. *Values for Tomorrow's Children.* New York: The Pilgrim Press, 1979.

--------. *Bringing up Children in the Christian Faith.* Minneapolis: Winston Press, 1980.

--------. *Living the Faith Community. The Church that makes a difference.* Minneapolis: Winston Press, 1985.

FAITH DEVELOPMENT

Dettoni, John M. Syllabus for '*Ecology of Faith Development*'. Pasadena: Fuller Theological Seminary, 1985.

Fowler, Jim; Keen, Sam; Berryman, Jim (eds). *Life Maps — Conversations on the Journey of Faith.* Waco, Texas: Word Inc., 1978.

Fowler, James W. *Stages of Faith. The Psychology of Human Development and the Quest for Meaning.* Melbourne: Dove Communications, 1981.

Groome, Thomas H. *Christian Religious Education.* Melbourne: Dove Communications, 1980.

Jones, Stephen D. *Faith Shaping.* Valley Forge: Judson Press, 1980.

Halverson, Delia Touchton. *Helping your Child Discover Faith.* Valley Forge: Judson Press, 1982.

GAMES

Trimby, Joyce (Compiler). *Cub Scout Games.* London: The Scout Association, (1972), 1985.

INTERGENERATIONAL ACTIVITIES

Griggs, Donald, and Griggs, Patricia. *Generations Learning Together. Learning Activities for Intergenerational Groups in the Church.* Livermore, C. A.: Griggs Educational Services, 1976.

Pearson, Keith and Allsop, Ian (eds). *Family Activities . . . a collection of resources for intergenerational groups* (Span Series). Melbourne: JBCE, 1977.

LEADERSHIP

Adair, John. *Effective Leadership. A modern guide to developing leadership skills.* London: Pan Books Ltd., 1983.

Blanchard, Kenneth and Lorber, Robert. *Putting the One Minute Manager to Work.* London: Fontana, 1983.

Blanchard, Kenneth; Zigarmi, Patricia; Zigarmi, Drea. *Leadership and the One Minute Manager.* London: Willow Books, 1985.

Johnson, Spenser. *The One Minute Father.* London: Columbus Books, 1983.

MORAL DEVELOPMENT

Brady, Laurie. *Children in Conflict. Problem Stories for Primary Grades.* Sydney: Dymock's Book Arcade Ltd.

--------. *Feel, Value, Act.* Sydney: Prentice Hall, Inc., 1979.

Cracknell, Vern. *To Find our Way. On promoting moral growth in the Scout Movement. A personal view.* Norwood: The Scout Association of Australia, S.A. Branch, 1985.

Duska, Ronald; Whelan, Mariellen. *Moral Development: A Guide to Piaget and Kohlberg.* New York: Paulist Press, 1975.

Galbraith, Ronald E. & Jones, Thomas M. *Moral Reasoning.* Minneapolis: Greenhave Press, 1976.

Hersh, Richard H; Paolitto, Diana Pritchard; Reimer, Joseph. *Promoting Moral Growth — from Piaget to Kohlberg.* London: Longman, 1979.

Hersh, Richard H; Miller, John P; Fielding, Glenn D. *Models of Moral Education. An Appraisal.* New York: Longman, 1980.

Lickona, Thomas. *Raising Good Children. From Birth through the Teenage Years.* Toronto: Bantam Books, 1983.

PRAYERS

Anderson, Geraldine (ed.). *Forty Devotions that Work with Youth,* Melbourne: JBCE, 1983.

Batchelor, Mary (Compiler). *The Lion Book of Children's Prayers.* Herts., Lion Publishing, (1977), 1983.

Edmond, Doug (ed.). *The Australian Scout Prayer Book.* Canberra: The Scout Association of Australia, 1984.

The Scout Association. *Scout Prayers.* London: The Scout Association, 1971.

PROGRAMS AND STRATEGIES

Anderson, Geraldine (ed.). *Fifty Fun Programs that Work with Youth.* Melbourne: JBCE, 1987.

Dieleman, Dale (Compiler). *Handbook on Service.* Michigan: Baker Book House, 1980.

Old, Margaret V. *Seven Plus.* London: Scripture Union, 1972.

Septima. *Something to do. 300 Games, Hobbies and Pastimes.* London: William Collins and Sons, (1966), 1971.

The Scout Association of Australia. *The Cub Scout Leaders Handbook.* Canberra: The Scout Association of Australia in conjunction with Horwitz Grahame Pty. Ltd., 1988.

Smyth, Glen. *What Will We Do on Friday Night?* Melbourne: JBCE, 1987.

REFERENCES, REPORTS AND DOCUMENTS

Bodycomb, John. *A Matter of Death and Life: The Future of Australia's Churches.* Melbourne: JBCE, 1986.

Cracknell, V. J. *Self-Directed Learning Programs for Leaders of Church Children's Clubs.* Dissertation submitted to Fuller Theological Seminary. Pasadena, Calif: 1988.

Dicks, Stewart; Mennill, Paul; Santor, Donald. *The Many Faces of Religion*. An Inquiry Approach. Canada: Ginn and Company, 1973.

Gill, David. General Secretary. *Minutes and Reports of the Fifth Assembly of the Uniting Church in Australia*. Melbourne: Uniting Church Press, 1988.

Tanner, Ian B. *A Handbook for Elders: within the Uniting Church in Australia*. Melbourne: Uniting Church Press, 1984.

Waller, Lynn. *International Children's Bible Dictionary*. Fort Worth: Sweet Publishing, 1987.

SONGS

Boucher, Rod and Rowland, Mike. *God Gives — Songs for Kids*. Blackwood: Rodan Publications, 1979.

Dyson, Mandy. *Bodyworks and other songs for God's kids*. Melbourne: JBCE, 1989.

Harrop, Beatrice. *Apusskidu. Songs for Children*. London: A. & C. Black Ltd., 1975.

Lomax, Alan. *The Penguin Book of American Folk Songs*. Ringwood: Penguin Books, 1964.

Manifold, John. *The Penguin Australian Song Book*. Ringwood: Penguin Books, 1964.

WORSHIP

Cracknell, Vern. *Scouts' Owns*. Canberra: The Scout Association of Australia, National Publications, 1985.

Ihli, Sister Jan. *Liturgy of the Word for Children*. New York: Paulist Press, 1979.